G000145443

MEAT AT ANY PRICE

by the same author

*

CHICKEN AND GAME

with Peggie Benton

FISH FOR ALL SEASONS

MEAT AT ANY PRICE

by Ninette Lyon

adapted from the French
and illustrated by

PEGGIE BENTON

FABER AND FABER
24 Russell Square
London

First published in 1963
by Faber and Faber Limited
24 Russell Square London W.C.1
First published in this edition 1969
Printed in Great Britain
by Latimer Trend & Co Ltd Whitstable

SBN (paper edition) 571 09078 8

SBN (cloth edition) 571 06944 4

CONTENTS

AUTHOR'S NOTE

Since the French butchers use quite a different system from the English, an entirely fresh approach to the cuts of meat has been necessary. This involved research which made considerable demands on the kindness and patience of a number of experts.

I should like to thank them all, and especially Mr. Ducat of Harrods and Mr. Padmore of John Gardner's.

INTRODUCTION

NINETTE LYON lives with her husband and three children at the top of a tall white house on the edge of the Parc Montsouris in Paris. The household is completed by a middle-aged dog, a tiny Spanish maid like a wrinkled walnut, and a stream of visitors. So it is not surprising that they overflow into the lower part of the house where Ninette's mother, Nadine Effront—slender, vital and half-Russian—shapes gold and shears and welds half-inch steel plate into intricate jewellery and dynamic modern sculptures.

Across the road, at a window, one glimpses a lean, white-haired figure—Braque, who has lived since the 'twenties in this quiet cul-de-sac.

In this atmosphere, it is not surprising that Ninette Lyon, besides being an inventive cook, is also a serious and very talented painter. They say that there is an affinity between painting and cooking, just as there is between music and mathematics.

Ninette Lyon, who was trained in domestic science, knows a great deal about meat. After finishing *Meat At Any Price* she was asked by the *Confédération Nationale de la Boucherie Française* to write the recipes for a pamphlet a million copies of which were distributed to butchers throughout the country.

Besides having a background of considerable theoretical knowledge, Ninette Lyon is a practical cook who understands shopping, budgeting and cooking for a household. She knows what it is like to come home tired after helping in her husband's office and to produce a meal for a family which, unlike many English ones, will not be satisfied with a frozen dinner or some hygienic tinned spaghetti. She knows, too, the agony of leaving a painting at its most interesting stage because it is lunch time and the children must be fed.

But, in her case, cooking has not been allowed to become just a chore. She enjoys experimenting with flavours just as she enjoys balancing colours. Many of the recipes in this book are present-day adaptations of classic dishes, but others are Ninette Lyon's own invention. All of them have gained something from the creative atmosphere in which they were evolved.

PEGGIE BENTON
Chelsea, 1962

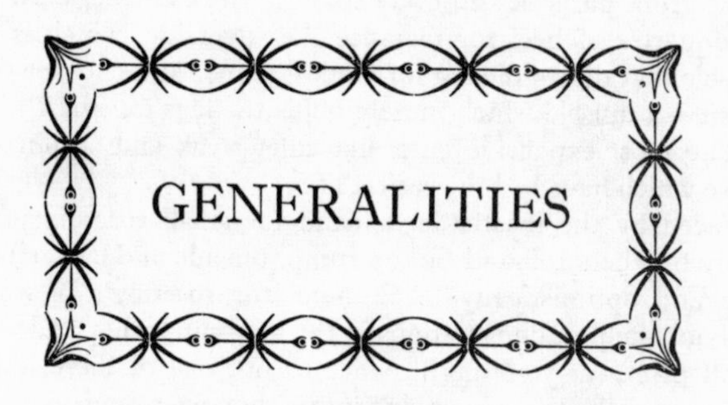

GENERALITIES

FIRST OF ALL, CHOOSE YOUR BUTCHER

THE butcher has two main problems: buying meat—and selling it.

Customers' tastes vary a little according to the district and the season of the year, and in certain areas cheap cuts are always popular. But there is an ever-increasing demand for dearer joints, tender roasting beef, legs of lamb and, above all, for steaks and chops, which are quick and easy to cook.

Now the butcher has to dispose of *all* his stock, and to come out even he can charge more for the popular cuts and reduce the price of the others. He can also make the best of as much meat as possible by cutting, trimming and even tenderizing it for use as roasts and grills.

It is difficult, perhaps impossible, for anyone who is not an expert to judge the quality of meat by its appearance. Roll of silverside, for example, can look like a wonderful piece of roasting beef but if you roast this joint it will be dry and tough. Braised, however, it will be excellent.

The ideal solution is to find a butcher whom you can trust, stick to him and be guided by his advice. It is to the butcher's advantage to give satisfaction to customers, who will in turn be loyal to him.

SHOPPING FOR MEAT

It is a safe rule that the harder a muscle has worked during the life of the animal the tougher it will be, so the really cheap cuts come from parts of the body like the neck and legs. In the hindquarter of beef for instance the silverside, which is the muscle that draws the leg forward, is leaner and cheaper than topside, a muscle which merely holds the legs together.

The most expensive cuts, like fillet steak and sirloin, are those which have had the easiest life.

Faced by the insatiable demand for small roasting joints many butchers roll and tie top rump, topside and even silverside and optimistically label them 'for roasting'. It would probably help public relations in the long run if they added, in small print, 'at your peril', since to put one of these joints, and especially the silverside, into a hot oven and expect a tender roast is asking for trouble.

Anyone who has suffered a number of disappointments with these 'roasting joints' is bound to come to the conclusion either that she is a poor cook or that the butcher is to blame —which is both damaging to morale and bad for business.

If you have a butcher you can trust, skip the next few paragraphs. He will value your custom, answer your questions, and take trouble to see that you do not buy the wrong cut of meat for your purpose.

If you have not yet found the ideal butcher and are shy of displaying your ignorance before a busy assistant and a long queue, you naturally hope to find some guidance in the shop window. So often, however, the labels only give vague indications that the meat is for roasting or frying, or that it is Scotch or imported.

Perhaps you turn to the pictures in the cookery book, but this is not always satisfactory because a photograph, even though highly coloured, can look so different from real meat.

Before giving up and joining the scramble for fillet steaks, try searching out a store where the cuts are clearly labelled. Some of the best self-service stores have quite explicit labels, 'Chuck', 'Brisket', 'Top Rump', and so on, and if you avoid rush hours you can put in some quiet study. You may not learn to distinguish on sight the difference between silverside and topside but you will learn to be more cautious about picking up that attractive little lean 'roasting joint' with the ruby flesh, and if you read this book you will have some idea of how to treat it if you should. (The self-service stores which are meticulous about labelling usually have their own butchers' shops and will be very happy, especially during quiet times, to answer your questions and to prepare just the piece of meat you are looking for. In this way, besides providing a discreet education they may well solve your meat buying problems for good.)

Note for family butchers. Please do not take these suggestions amiss. If the labels in *your* window really tell the customer what she is buying she can browse quietly outside the shop before making a decision—and this is a great help to the shy and the inexperienced, as well as to the keen cook. If it is really too complicated to print tickets for 'Flank', 'Fore rib' and so on, as my favourite self-service store does, then a few tickets marked 'pot roasting or braising' for the secondary joints would save a great deal of disappointment and consumer unrest.

FRENCH CUTS OF MEAT

French butchers use more care and skill in cutting up meat than ordinary butchers in this country, but however meticulously an English butcher may work there are certain French cuts which are impossible for him to produce, since the carcases are divided differently at the *abattoirs*. You might just as well ask a tailor to produce a raglan overcoat from a garment already cut with divided sleeves.

Just as in this country, the method of cutting meat varies from one region of France to another. The charts drawn up for the guidance of the Common Market have used the Parisian system for France and the London and Home Counties method for the United Kingdom. These are the systems which we have followed in the hope that they will, in time, be generally adopted.

There are, in London at least, a number of Continental butchers who have always sold French cuts of meat. Following Harrods' lead an increasing number of British butchers are beginning to sell them too, though in some cases the only thing which is French about such cuts is the name—frequently mis-spelt.

In order that you may have some understanding of *boucherie* meat, and also be able to find a substitute for the cut mentioned in a French recipe, we are giving a list of the French cuts most usually sold here and their nearest English equivalents.

The introduction of French cuts, though it is an excellent idea, tends to complicate an already intricate branch of shopping. To add to the confusion, customers often ask for meat by the name of the dish they wish to cook, and butchers are consequently beginning to label meat in this way. You may be offered 'bœuf à la mode' or 'blanquette de veau', which could simply be more tempting names for stewing steak or pie veal, though in France bœuf à la mode is usually made from topside or top rump, whilst blanquette of veal is best if you use meat from the shoulder or the knuckle.

BEEF

French Cut	Nearest English Equivalent
Gîte à la noix	Roll of silverside
Tendre de tranche	Best part of the topside. A muscle rimmed with fat, and seamless
Flanchet	Top rump, or thick flank
Bavette	Skirt
Rumstek	Rump steak
Filet	Fillet
Faux or contre-filet	Eye of the sirloin
Côte de bœuf	Wing rib
Entrecôte	Cut from wing ribs. (Properly from between the ribs)
Plat de côte	Forequarter flank
Tendron	Brisket

VEAL

French Cut	Nearest English Equivalent
Jarret	Knuckle of veal
Quasi	The rump

Noix	Topside of beef
Noix pâtissière	Thick flank
Longe	Loin
Carré	Best end of neck
Côtelettes	Loin chops
Côtelettes premières	The four cutlets from the best end of neck nearest the loin
Côtelettes secondes	The four cutlets from the best end of neck furthest from the loin
Bas de carré	Scrag
Epaule	Shoulder
Escalope	Fairly thin slice of lean meat cut on the bias, usually from the leg or loin
Médaillon	An escalope which is round in shape and often cut from the loin
Grenadin	A small steak cut from the leg, thicker than a médaillon
Fricandeau	A small plump muscle from the leg

MUTTON AND LAMB

French Cut	Nearest English Equivalent
Gigot	Leg
Selle	Saddle
Filet	Loin
Côtelettes dans le filet	Loin chops
Carré	Best end of neck
Côtelettes premières	The four cutlets from the best end of neck nearest the loin
Côtelettes secondes	The four cutlets from the best end of neck furthest from the loin
Haut de côtelettes	Between breast and best end of neck
Collet or collier	Neck or scrag
Poitrine	Breast
Noisettes	Made by boning and slicing the best end of neck. (Sometimes the adjoining flap is wrapped round the noisettes to keep them in shape)

PORK

French Cut	Nearest English Equivalent
Jambonneau	Hind and fore knuckle
Jambon	Upper part of hind leg
Pointe de filet	Hind loin
Filet	Centre or middle loin
Carré	Best end of neck
Côtelettes	Chops
Epaule	Shoulder
Echine	Spare ribs
Palette	Blade bone
Jambon de devant	Hand and spring
Poitrine	Belly
Tête or hure	Head
Pied	Foot
Lard gras or bardière	Back pork fat used for larding and barding (p. 34)

HOW TO KEEP MEAT

The length of time for which meat should be hung varies considerably according to the conditions. Meat which is cooked too soon after slaughtering is tough and tasteless though the same meat, properly hung, will be tender and well-flavoured. (Offal, on the other hand, *must* be eaten fresh.)

In large towns meat is hung in special cool chambers and afterwards distributed over a wide area. In the country, where such services are not always available, meat is sometimes sold too fresh.

Ventilation is an essential condition for proper hanging, which cannot be carried out successfully in a domestic refrigerator. Meat may even be hung until the surface is covered with a black crust. This crust is cut off just before cooking, and the underlying meat has the most wonderful flavour and texture.

In some countries, such as Spain and Italy, the hanging of meat is not generally understood whilst in others, particularly the United States, where the consumption of meat is very high, it has been carried to perfection.

Once meat has been brought home it should be unwrapped

and put in the refrigerator, ideally in the chill tray, or failing this in the coldest part of the shelf so that it remains at a temperature of about 35–50° F (Centigrade, about 2–4°). The surface of the meat which is exposed to the air will darken, but this does not matter. If you wish to preserve its colour sprinkle the meat with monosodium glutamate. (This is on sale in most good grocer's shops under a trade name such as ACCENT.)

Offal should be laid on foil (not greaseproof paper, which sticks), and loosely bunched so that air can reach it without juice trickling out.

KEEPING TIMES FOR MEAT IN A REFRIGERATOR

Beef and Mutton

Joints	up to 6 days
Steaks	,, 5 days
Stewing meat, cut up	,, 4 days
Minced meat	,, 2 days
Offal	,, 24 hours

Veal and Lamb

Joints	up to 6 days
Chops, escalopes, etc.	,, 4 days
Cut-up meat	2 to 3 days
Offal	24 hours

Pork

Joints	up to 6 days
Chops, fillet slices, etc.	,, 4 days
Salt pork	,, 8 days
Sliced ham	,, 5 days
Whole ham	,, 8 days
Fresh pure pork sausages	,, 3 days

NOTE: All types of minced meat should be eaten as soon as possible after mincing.

IF YOU HAVE NO REFRIGERATOR. Keep the meat in a cool place free from flies and sheltered from direct light. It should be protected by cellophane or foil, but not tightly wrapped, and eaten as soon as possible.

IF YOU WANT TO SAVE TIME, and have a large refrigerator, you can, by shopping intelligently, lay in sufficient meat for a whole week. For instance, you could provide for the first day liver, kidney, brains, or one of the other offals; for the second, minced meat; the third, a casserole; the fourth a grill; the fifth a roast; the sixth a braise or pot-au-feu, and for the seventh a dish created with some meat which has been left from a previous meal. Once meat has been cooked it can be kept for two days longer.

You can also buy a single large joint and slice pieces off it for various purposes. Ribs and legs lend themselves very well to this treatment.

DOWN WITH OLD BOOTS

Though the cheaper cuts of meat are not so tender or juicy as those of the highest quality they are just as nourishing. Moreover, tenderness is largely the result of skilful cooking, and the finest meat, badly cooked, can turn into shoe leather without the butcher being in any way to blame.

The meat from one of the more active muscles of an elderly animal, minced or simmered, can be delicious provided it is carefully prepared, but if it is to make a successful dish you must understand the nature of the cut you have bought and know what you have a right to expect from it. The tables at the beginning of each section are a guide to the characteristics of the various cuts.

Cooking temperatures are important too. Meat contains albumen and at 175° F this coagulates and hardens. When meat is 'seared' at a lively heat this forms a coating which helps to prevent the juices from escaping. Once this coating is formed you should not continue cooking at too high a temperature, since the outside of the meat will burn while the inside remains underdone. Moreover, meat which is cooked at a moderate temperature shrinks less.

Meat should be taken out of the refrigerator at least half an hour before cooking so that it is thoroughly thawed, since if it is very cold the juices will be lost more rapidly during cooking. Some American cookery books advocate putting hard-frozen meat straight into the oven, but this procedure is probably designed to save time rather than to produce a better roast.

The angle at which meat is sliced can be important. Escalopes cut across the grain at an angle of 45° are more tender and less likely to tear. The Chinese, whose food is prepared with meticulous care and cooked only briefly, slice even vegetables diagonally to give them a more delicate texture.

Some butchers use tenderizing machines on second-grade steak. The tiny spikes of the 'needle machines' break up the fibres of the meat, but the lacerations allow juice to escape during cooling. The American 'lace machines', which are also in use here, give the meat rather an unpleasant texture. You will recognize steak which has been through such a machine by the regular pattern on the surface and the lacy appearance.

Tenderizing powders and liquids are on sale in many shops but these leave the meat a little slimy and a far better result is obtained by choosing your cuts carefully and cooking them in a suitable way.

THE FIVE MAIN WAYS OF COOKING MEAT

ROASTING. True roasting, on a spit by an open fire, requires too much fuel, space and labour for present-day conditions. Nowadays, meat is usually baked in the oven. For this process, only tender joints with a fair proportion of fat are suitable. The exact method used varies according to the meat concerned and to individual preferences. You will find further notes on roasting at the beginning of each section.

COOKING IN WATER. Salted meat and the tougher portions of an animal such as the head and feet are usually boiled, at least as a preliminary. Stews should never boil, just simmer.

BRAISING. After browning in hot fat the meat is cooked very slowly with a small quantity of liquid such as stock or wine. Daubes, carbonades and all the delightful dishes which come under the heading of braises must never boil, but simmer so gently that the surface of the liquid only shows a slight tremor.

GRILLING is cooking by radiant heat, nowadays usually under a fixed gas or electric grill, though the original method with glowing charcoal or a red-hot fire gives a far better flavour. The meat once seared is cooked in its own juice. This method is only satisfactory for small and tender cuts.

A SAUTÉ, like a grill, is a quick way of cooking tender meat, which is 'seized' in a little very hot fat and cooked quickly in the pan. (It is confusing that the name sauté is also applied to veal ragoûts the meat for which, unlike that for blanquettes, is first browned in fat.)

COOKING TIMES AND TEMPERATURES

Cooking is not an exact science so the indications we give can only be a guide, never a guarantee of success. To begin with, the best cooks disagree about details and even, sometimes, about basic methods. Even supposing they were all of one mind, there are so many imponderables.

Different makes of cookers behave in different ways. Oven indicators are not always reliable. Some ovens are much hotter at the top than the bottom whilst others maintain a more even heat throughout. As electric cookers grow older the heat of the boiling plates sometimes fluctuates more sharply with the variations in current.

A great deal of success in cooking depends on knowing your own apparatus and the materials with which you are working, and using observation and common sense.

We try to give useful guidance. If things, as we hope, go well you will enjoy the credit. If they go a little less well, remember *we* have done our best.

It is difficult to give precise details about roasting a joint, since so many factors are involved. Of two joints weighing the same the one with the most compact shape will take longer to cook as there will be less surface exposed to the heat.

Meat with bone will require a few minutes less per pound than boned meat, and fat meat will cook more quickly than lean, since both bone and fat are excellent conductors of heat. Some people like their meat rare, others prefer it well done and here, too, cooking times will vary.

You may find it worth while to invest in a meat thermometer. This should be inserted in the thickest part of the meat before it is put in the oven. Using a skewer or pointed knife make a slit for the thermometer and be sure that the bulb does not rest upon bone or fat. The following thermometer readings should show when the meat is done: Beef, rare, 140° F (60° C); beef, medium, 160° F (71° C); beef, well done, 170° F (76° C); lamb and mutton, 175° F (80° C); veal, 170° F (76° C); pork, 185° F (85° C). Unfortunately, not all thermometers are equally accurate.

It used to be thought that if meat were seared at a high temperature the juices would be sealed in, but research has shown that the seal is never complete. The high temperature causes the moisture in the meat to boil and escape as steam through the 'pores' which remain open, and the meat shrinks and dries quite unnecessarily. In spite of this many people still prefer to sear their joints at about 425° F (220° C, Gas 7) for the first quarter of an hour and then lower the heat to about 355° F (180° C, Gas 4). Others raise the temperature for the last quarter of an hour in order to brown the joint.

The modern method of roasting is to cook all joints at a low temperature, and one big catering company is even experimenting with roasting meat at 200° F (which is below the lowest setting on the average stove) in order to avoid shrinking and wastage, and to produce really juicy, well-flavoured roasts.

For stuffed joints remember to add about 5–10 minutes per lb to the roasting time.

At a low temperature basting with fat is not necessary and may even do more harm than good, since roasting meat is protected from the heat of the oven by an envelope of steam. If you baste with fat which is at a far higher temperature, you merely break the steam seal.

Basting with liquids such as stock and wine, which remain

at a lower temperature than fat, helps to keep the drier types of meat juicy and to improve their flavour.

Before roasting a joint wipe it with a damp cloth but never wash it, as the moisture will increase the cooking time besides hardening the outside.

When the joint is ready, turn off the heat and leave it to 'rest' for a few minutes in the oven.

If you have neither a temperature dial nor a thermometer for your oven a piece of white paper will give a useful rough guide. Shut in the oven for one minute it will give the following indications:

In a moderate oven, about 355° F (180° C, Gas 4)
the paper will turn yellow
" hot " " 425° F (220° C, Gas 7)
the paper browns
" very hot " " 470° F (245° C, Gas 9)
the paper turns black

Stews and Braises

Here is an approximate guide to the times required for stewing and braising. These vary according to the quality of the meat. Always have a little time in hand in case the meat should prove unexpectedly tough and never try to hurry things on by raising the heat.

Pot-au-feu and tough cuts for boiling	3 to 5	hours
Braised beef and daubes	3 to 4	"
Braised veal and blanquettes of veal or lamb	1½	"
Stewed mutton	1½ to 2	"

Meat Sauté on a Pan

If you like your meat underdone and juicy, turn it as soon as moisture begins to gather in beads on the surface—and only turn it once, being careful not to pierce the meat as you do so.

Grilling

Most gas or electric grills are arranged so that by varying either the position of the pan or the height of the rack the surface of the meat is about 2–2½ inches from the source of heat. In these conditions brown your meat on both sides at full heat, then lower the heat to finish, turning the meat once.

Steaks will need about 8–15 minutes in all, depending on their thickness and the degree to which you like them cooked; cutlets about 7–10 minutes; chops 10–20 minutes.

If you wish to grill your food over an open fire:

—first make a good blaze and then put the charcoal on top

—wait until the flames have died down and the coals are glowing

—see that the meat is far enough from the embers to ensure that it is not seared by flames caused by the dripping fat

—never pierce the surface of the meat: turn it with tongs or hold it in a double grill.

Barbecues are a form of grill. Pieces of meat marinaded in a piquant sauce are cooked slowly over a fire, usually of charcoal. It is said that barbecues were introduced to America by French-Canadian hunters who roasted whole animals 'de barbe à queue' over pits of glowing coals.

USEFUL HINTS AND BASIC PRINCIPLES

In making a braise or a stew the quantity of liquid required depends partly on the size of the casserole. If this is too large the liquid will dry up more quickly. This difficulty can be avoided if you have two different sizes of heavy flameproof casseroles with tight-fitting lids. Ideally, the larger one should be oval.

The lid of your casserole must be very heavy to prevent the escape of steam and preferably shaped, so that the liquid which collects falls back on to the food and keeps it moist.

If the dish becomes too dry add some more *hot* liquid. With a tightly-closed casserole evaporation is reduced to a minimum and no extra liquid should be needed.

If the sauce is too thin you can raise the heat a little and leave the lid off the pan for a time, or else thicken the liquid. (A teaspoonful of arrowroot mixed with a tablespoon of cold water makes the sauce fuller but not pasty.)

If you use flour for thickening work it into a roux with warm butter. Be careful that the sauce is not boiling when you thicken it, or lumps will form.

A casserole dish is excellent warmed up, and it can be varied or made to go further by adding fresh vegetables. Avoid those like Brussels sprouts or turnips with too strong a flavour.

Even if you are only cooking for two it is always better to roast or braise at least two pounds of meat, as a smaller joint will be drier and less tender. You can easily plan a second meal with what is left.

When you are grilling meat always pre-heat the grill and leave the door of the compartment open. (Many stoves are arranged so that it is not possible to close the grill whilst it is in use.)

If your recipe includes bacon it is wise to test it. If too salty, plunge the bacon for a moment in boiling water, then drain and dry it before cooking. This also removes the saltpetre which spoils the colour of certain dishes.

Be cautious with the salt if bacon or anchovies are included in a recipe.

If you add salt before simmering a dish remember that the liquid will be reduced by evaporation, and the taste of the salt will become more pronounced.

Egg is largely composed of albumen and coagulates very quickly on contact with heat. When food is fried in egg and breadcrumbs a crust is formed which prevents the fat from soaking in. Be sure that the *whole* surface of the food is coated with beaten egg.

Once you have added cream or mustard see that a sauce does not boil. It will then remain smooth and creamy.

Parsley and herbs which are chopped on a board, or inside a glass using a pair of scissors, are crisper than those which are put through a small chopping machine. The machine does, however, save valuable time.

If you are adding onions or shallots to a stuffing they should be parboiled first, or chopped and softened in butter.

GARNISH GRACEFULLY

You can cut down your meat bill by buying the cheaper cuts, or by providing a smaller quantity of meat and making up for this with a nourishing soup or pudding, but do be generous with your imagination. Meat doesn't *have* to be accompanied by potatoes, boiled cabbage or frozen peas. There are all sorts of delightful herbs and vegetables in the shops and you will find suggestions in the cooking notes at the beginning of the sections dealing with the various kinds of meat.

Instead of potatoes try noodles tossed in butter; dried chestnuts soaked and pressure-cooked (or fresh ones if you have the patience to skin them); butter beans with chopped parsley; French bread rubbed with garlic, buttered and crisped in the oven; rice with a dusting of paprika or curry powder. Any of these go beautifully with meat, especially if you add a tossed green salad.

There are some classic French accompaniments which, served with your roasts and grills, will turn a family meal into a feast. Some of these are described below, and may also help you to cope with menus written in French.

A l'ancienne: quenelles of chicken, truffles, mushrooms, prawns, sweetbreads.
Boulangère: sliced potatoes and onion rings mixed and cooked in the oven together with the meat.
Bouquetière: small mounds of vegetables—carrots, young turnips, button onions, French beans, asparagus tips, peas, cauliflower, potatoes cut and shaped like large olives, arranged round the meat and sprinkled with melted butter and finely chopped fresh herbs.
Bourguignonne: small onions and button mushrooms sautéd with chopped bacon. The bottom of the pan is deglazed (p. 35) with red wine.
Catalane: aubergines sautéd in olive oil, rice and tomato sauce.
Châtelaine: chestnut purée, onions and noisette potatoes.
Clamart: peas and, if possible, globe artichokes sprinkled with melted butter.

Conti: lentil croquettes, noisette potatoes, madeira sauce (p. 20).
Dubarry: heads of cauliflower covered with sauce mornay (p. 202) and browned with a sprinkling of breadcrumbs.
Financière: quenelles of veal, cock's combs, mushrooms, truffles, sweetbreads.
Forestière: mushrooms sautéd in butter and noisette potatoes.
Henry IV: (for tournedos) served on artichoke hearts and covered with béarnaise sauce (p. 198).
Mirabeau: green olives, fillets of anchovy, chopped tarragon.
Niçoise: baked tomatoes sprinkled with breadcrumbs and chopped garlic, French beans, anchovies, olives and fried croûtons.
Orientale: tomatoes stuffed with rice; peppers.
Parisienne: potatoes, braised lettuce, artichoke hearts.
Provençale: aubergines and tomatoes sprinkled with breadcrumbs and browned, French beans, fried croûtons: the whole sprinkled with chopped garlic and finely minced parsley.
Richelieu: tomatoes and mushrooms dressed with browned breadcrumbs and butter, braised lettuce, potatoes.
Rossini: slices of foie gras sautéd in butter, shavings of truffle.
Saint-Germain: purée of peas.
Vert pré: straw potatoes, watercress, maître d'hôtel butter (p. 201).
Viennoise: Yolks and whites of hard-boiled eggs chopped separately, anchovies, capers and a slice of lemon, minced parsley. (Though less elegant, a segment of lemon which can be squeezed is far more convenient than a slice.)

THE INVALUABLE POTATO

Potatoes are the most usual and, if well prepared, the best of all accompaniments to meat. Here are some alternatives to the ordinary boiled or mashed spuds:

Allumettes. Cut into sticks like large matches and fried.
Boulangère. Onions and potatoes cut in slices and baked with the joint.

Château. Cut and shaped like large olives; blanched, buttered and cooked in the oven, or sautéd in butter.

Chips. Chipped potatoes require no description in England (where they are sometimes even served with spaghetti!) but the French author describes 'pommes chips' as potatoes cut into fine slices and fried.

Dauphine. Potato purée mixed with yolk of egg and choux paste, formed into croquettes, egg-and-breadcrumbed and fried.

Dauphinoise. Sliced potatoes arranged in a buttered fireproof dish, well sprinkled with milk, and covered with grated cheese.

Fondant. Shaped like large olives and poached in chicken broth, using a casserole with a tight-fitting lid.

Gratin. Potato purée into which you have stirred butter and beaten yolks of eggs; cooked in a fireproof dish beneath a golden crust of butter, breadcrumbs and cheese.

Lyonnaise. Sliced and cooked in butter, sprinkled with finely chopped parsley.

Noisette. Scooped into the shape of hazel nuts with a potato cutter, cooked in butter which is just beginning to brown, and sprinkled with chopped fresh herbs.

Paille. Cut into the finest straws and fried.

Persillé. New potatoes cooked in bouillon and dusted with chopped parsley.

Pont-Neuf. These are similar to English chips.

Provençale. Sautéd in oil with as much garlic as your social life allows.

Sauté. Raw or cooked potatoes cut in slices or fingers and sautéd in fat.

COOKING FATS

It is the fat used in cooking which, more than anything else, gives the characteristic flavour to regional dishes. The taste of olive oil permeates Mediterranean food while in Northern France and Belgium butter is characteristic. In Périgord and Alsace goose fat flavours the cooking, but lard is used for the specialities of the Charente region.

The choice of fat for meat dishes is largely a question of taste and habit so, except in the case of regional recipes, we leave the choice to you. Oil, butter, margarine or dripping can generally be used with equal success.

Too much fat is indigestible and you should be careful to skim off any surplus before a dish is served. Meat requires very little fat for browning provided you put only a few slices into the pan at a time.

Since fat congeals rapidly it is important to heat all meat plates and dishes. (An Englishman we know, who lives in Spain, struggled for years against icy dishes and congealing gravy. Finally, his favourite restaurant agreed to pander to his eccentricity, and now they even bring him the bill on a hot plate!)

Butter. Uncooked butter is rich in vitamins and calories and is very digestible. Since butter burns at a low temperature it is wise, when heating it to smoking point, to add a little vegetable oil. This reduces the risk of burning, which makes butter both bitter and indigestible.

Margarine. Margarine is a mixture of vegetable and animal oils blended with soured skimmed milk to give a butter flavour. By law, all the margarine made in this country must contain vitamins A and D, and whilst the vitamin content of butter varies according to the time of year and the way in which the cows are fed, that of margarine is constant and often higher. Its caloric content is the same as that of butter.

Cooking Oils. These are of vegetable origin and are made from olives, ground nuts, maize, rape and various seeds.

Olive oil, which is the most expensive, varies in flavour according to the region from which it comes and the degree to which it has been refined. The oil from Provence is the lightest and most delicate, though some now exported from Italy and Spain is almost as good. If you enjoy using olive oil it is well worth buying a gallon tin and decanting it a bottle at a time. The oil will keep perfectly in a cool place and, bought in bulk, the finest quality only costs about 5*s.* a pint, which is very little more than ordinary cooking oil.

If you buy olive oil in small bottles, then it is a considerable economy to use one of the other vegetable oils for cooking. These are quite tasteless and only burn at 535° F (280° Centigrade) whereas olive oil burns at 482° F (250° Centigrade).

Lard is made of fat, usually from the back of the pig. Its flavour suits both pork and mutton. Fleed or leaf lard (so-called because of the leaf-like pattern which forms on the surface of the fat as it cools) is made from the flare fat round the kidney. It is extremely fatty and should be used sparingly. Leaf lard burns at about 375° F (190° Centigrade) and ordinary lard at only 338° F (170° Centigrade).

Dripping. The dripping from roasts (except mutton, which has rather a strong flavour) and the fat skimmed from stews may be melted, strained and poured into a bowl. After cooling for 24 hours pierce a couple of holes in the fat and drain off any liquid, or better still, lift the fat and scrape off any burnt particles which have collected beneath. Keep the dripping in a cool, dry place.

Goose Fat. In order to have a stock of goose fat, which is excellent for cooking or spreading on bread (children love it) choose a plump goose and cook it slowly in a moderate oven. Mix the fat with a teaspoonful of coarse salt to each pound and pour it into small jars. If stored in a cool place it will keep for a year.

THE STORE CUPBOARD

If you wish to try our recipes or make experiments of your own you will need, besides the usual salt, pepper, mustard, cloves, nutmeg and so on:

Fillets of anchovy, salted or preserved in oil.

Packets of dried mushrooms. (Soak them in tepid water for an hour before cooking. The water can be used in making a sauce or a soup.)

Little tins of tomato purée. (The smallest size holds about 3 tablespoons.)

Packets of grated parmesan cheese. (Freshly grated parmesan has a far better flavour, but the packets are useful in an emergency.)

Cubes of chicken and beef bouillon. (The Swiss Knorr cubes with their delicate aromas of herbs and vegetables are especially good.)

French mustard. This is made in a variety of flavours, and there is also a light champagne mustard which is sold in a convenient tube.

Curry powder. Different makes of curry powder vary in pungency and flavour. You may find your favourite by experiment, or decide to keep two or three in the cupboard.

Paprika. It is worth while buying genuine Hungarian paprika which is sold in the best stores.

Cayenne pepper.

Powdered ginger. This is useful not only for cakes and puddings, but it gives a spark to certain meat dishes and blends well with curry. Ginger is delicious with melon.

Tiny dried peppers. These are now sold in cellophane packets in many self-service stores.

Saffron (indispensable if you are making *risotto milanese* or *bouillabaisse*).

Black and green olives.

Cinammon. Powdered cinammon is sometimes adulterated or made from inferior bark, so it is more satisfactory to use the natural cinammon sticks, where possible.

Some bottled sauces such as mushroom, horse-radish and Worcestershire, tomato ketchup and soya extract. (A few drops of soya extract will heighten the flavour of a sauce, soup or salad, and is particularly good with vegetable combinations.)

Dried herbs. Fresh herbs are always better than dried ones but, except for mint and parsley, these are not easy to find in an ordinary shop, and even those fortunate enough to have a herb garden will be obliged to use dried herbs during the winter.

A small stock of dried herbs makes a useful basis for experiment. You could start with thyme (which with parsley and bay leaves makes the traditional bouquet garni); mixed sweet herbs (usually marjoram, savory, thyme, parsley and celery);

an Italian blend usually containing oregano, thyme, parsley, basil, sage, bay leaves and spices, for flavouring *pasta* sauce and *pizzas*. If you enjoy using herbs there are many other delightful varieties on the market. One of the most rewarding is basil, which is delicious with tomatoes, salads and omelets.

One point is worth remembering. Unless dried herbs are kept in air-tight containers, and preferably in the dark, they quickly lose their flavour, so avoid paper and cardboard packets. Also, unless you are cooking for a large family, it is better value to buy small quantities, which are more expensive weight for weight but do not last so long that they become tasteless, and finally have to be thrown away. The Chiltern Herb Farms put up excellent small glass containers with sprinkler tops and pleasantly designed labels describing each herb and its uses. These herbs are green-dried by a special process which gives them a particularly lively flavour.

A bottle of madeira, marsala or sherry and one of brandy or rum. If these are used only in the kitchen they will last a surprisingly long time. There are about fifty-five tablespoons in each bottle. If you decide to use a French brandy at 32*s*. 6*d*. a bottle for cooking, a tablespoon (which is often all that a recipe requires) will cost you 7*d*. This is not ruinous, though it will not improve your temper to be reminded that about 5*d*. of your money is going to the Customs and Excise.

You will also need red and white wine, and possibly cider. Many husbands are glad to hand over unfinished wine to the cooking department, or you may poach the odd glass from one of your favourite bottles. If you buy cheap wine specially for cooking the chances are that it will go sour long before it is finished and the result in any case will not be so good.

Wherever flavours are concerned it is wise to buy the best, and usually in the smallest available quantities.

It is really worth while investing in pepper and salt mills. Ordinary ground pepper is frequently stale and sometimes adulterated (ground date stones being one of the strange things which creep in), and can never compare with the tang of freshly-milled peppercorns. Coarse sea salt ground in a mill has a far more lively flavour than the usual cooking or table varieties.

SOME THINGS YOU SHOULD KNOW

Measuring is Important

Throughout this book we have used the following equivalent measures:

1 glass = 1 cup = 7 fluid ounces
1 tablespoon of butter = ½ ounce
1 tablespoon of flour = ⅓ ounce
1 cup of minced cooked meat = about ½ pound

Some Meat Cooking Terms

Back pork fat: a layer of fat which lies beneath the skin covering the back of a pig.

Bain-marie. Delicate sauces are usually made in small pans standing in a water bath or bain-marie whose temperature should not exceed about 185° F (85° C), or well below boiling point. Sauces can also be kept warm in a bain-marie provided the temperature does not rise above 140° F (60° C). Traditionally, the bain-marie is a large copper pan, but a baking tin makes quite a useful substitute.

A bain-marie can be used in the oven when making custards and creams.

It is dangerous to use a double saucepan instead of a bain-marie when making delicate sauces, as the water can so easily boil unobserved and curdle the sauce.

Bards. These are thin slices cut from the back pork fat and used to wrap round the drier or more delicate kinds of meat, game or poultry during cooking to baste and protect them. Bards are usually held in place with string.

Blanching. To cleanse sweetbreads, brains, heads, etc. and to make the flesh firmer and easier to handle, they are put into cold salted water, brought to the boil and simmered for 2 to 3 minutes. Other foodstuffs are plunged into boiling water to improve their flavour, texture or appearance. Both processes are known as blanching.

Bouquet garni: a small bunch of herbs used to flavour soups, stews, etc. which is removed before serving. It usually consists of parsley (the stalks alone being sufficient), thyme and a bay leaf. More elaborate combinations, including chervil, tarragon, basil, celery, savory, rosemary and even orange peel are used for certain dishes, but care must be taken that the flavour of the various herbs does not become overpowering.

Court-bouillon. Various kinds of court-bouillon are used for cooking meat, fish, vegetables, etc. The simplest form used in meat cookery consists of carrots, onions, peppercorns and garlic simmered for 15 minutes in salted water. Calf's head and some other forms of offal are cooked in a white court-bouillon (or '*blanc*'). This is made by mixing a good tablespoonful of flour into each quart of water which is then strained and brought to the boil with a tablespoonful of vinegar, salt, an onion studded with two cloves, and a bouquet garni.

Deglazing: adding liquid to a pan in which food has cooked, in order to make a sauce.

Egg-and-breadcrumb: to coat food first in flour, then beaten egg and finally breadcrumbs.

Flambé. Food is flambé by pouring over it burning brandy or sherry which has first been warmed in a spoon or small saucepan. Some recipes require wine to be flambé to remove any harsh flavour. In this case the wine is brought to the boil, set alight and boiled until the flames have died down.

Larding. Strips of fat are threaded into the meat with a special larding needle, or they can be pushed into small slits made with the point of a knife. This prevents the meat from drying during cooking and provides extra richness. Larding is not a very easy job and is better done by the butcher. If you are doing it yourself be careful to see that the single 'stitches', which should be at regular intervals, go with the grain of the meat and that the small ends which protrude are of equal length.

Lardoons: the strips of fat used for larding. These are of varying length and thickness and are cut, ideally, from dried salted back pork fat. It is much easier to cut the fat if it is put into the refrigerator for a time before being used. (The French also apply the expression '*lardons*' to streaky pork or bacon cut in dice and fried golden-brown.

Poaching: cooking in liquid so gently that the surface only just quivers.

Reducing: heating a liquid over a quick fire with the lid off the pan, so that the quantity is reduced by evaporation.

Searing or Seizing: exposing the surface of meat to a high temperature at the outset of cooking. This forms a crisp crust which was formerly believed to seal in the juices. After searing, cooking is continued at a lower temperature.

Simmering: cooking in a liquid over a low heat so that the surface is gently agitated and bubbles may rise at one point (as distinct from the fast movement and overall bubbling of *boiling* liquid, and the almost imperceptible movement of poaching).

How to make a success of our recipes

Our recipes are printed in two separate colums.

The *ingredients* are shown in the left-hand column in the order in which they are used.

The *various operations* are described in the right-hand column as they occur.

All the recipes are meant for 4 people unless otherwise stated. To make your choice easier they are grouped according to the kind of meat used and the method of cooking. We show whether each recipe is:

expensive
moderately expensive
economical
very economical

We have, deliberately, described few very expensive dishes. If you are feeling extravagant consult the list of classic French garnishes on p. 27. These will turn your roasts and grills into very special dishes.

Meat tables

At the beginning of each section there are tables showing the characteristics of the various cuts, and some brief notes on the usual methods of cooking them. Many different systems of cutting and local names are in use in various parts of the British Isles. We have used the system applied in London and the Home Counties which has been adopted for Common Market discussions. In order that cuts can be identified in other parts of the country we have described their position.

The Index and the table of contents

If you want to choose a recipe to suit your budget consult the *index:* the recipes are grouped according to their cost.

If you want to choose a dish for any particular meat—beef, veal, mutton, lamb, pork and so on—look at the *table of contents.*

USUAL CUTS OF BEEF IN LONDON AND THE HOME COUNTIES

Cut	Position	Characteristics	Cooking Suggestions
Leg (Shank, Hind Shin)	Lower part of hind leg.	Very economical cut. The flavour is excellent and there is little fat. The gristle and sinew become tender and gelatinous with long, slow cooking. The bones contain marrow.	Used for stews, braises and beef tea.
Thick (or Goose **Skirt**	Part of inner muscle of belly wall adjoining rump.	Only ox skirts are sold. Those of smaller animals are left attached to joint. Thick skirt is cheap, coarse-grained but well-flavoured.	The best quality can be scored across and grilled or fried. Generally skirt is used for puddings and stews.
Thin Skirt	The muscular part of the diaphragm.	This is not always easy to buy.	Usually stewed, and has a fine flavour.
Body Skirt	The pillars of the diaphragm.	Most butchers seem shocked at being asked for this. It is usually left attached to the loin, or trimmed away.	Excellent for puddings and has the finest flavour of the three skirts.
Topside (or Round)	Inside of back leg.	Fairly expensive. Very lean and inclined to be dry. Is sometimes sold as buttock steak.	Makes excellent pot roasts, stews and braises. If used as steak, should be marinaded before cooking.

BEEF (continued)

Cut	Position	Characteristics	Cooking Suggestions
Silverside (Round)	The outside thigh muscle.	A little cheaper than topside and tougher, as this muscle works harder. The meat is lean and rather dry.	Traditionally salted and boiled. If boned and rolled for pot roasting, etc., the gristle should be removed and extra fat added. Makes good *bœuf à la mode* after larding.
Aitchbone	Pelvic region.	Rather a large joint, but economical if bought whole. Usually boned, or half-boned, for convenience in carving. Sometimes sold as an extension of the silverside.	Usually roasted, but sometimes salted and boiled.
Top Rump (or Thick Flank)	Muscle at the front of the thigh.	Medium in price between topside and silverside, and an economical buy.	Best quality can be roasted with a little water in the pan, or cut into steaks and fried slowly. It is better braised or stewed.
Thin (or Hindquarter) **Flank**	Lower portion of the belly wall.	Cheaper joint with rather a lot of fat. Is much improved if inner skin, bone and gristle are removed before rolling. Can also be cut up for stews, pies and puddings.	If left whole, may be salted and boiled, or used for stews or braises. If cut up for pies, etc. it is better mixed with some leaner meat.

BEEF (continued)

Cut	Position	Characteristics	Cooking Suggestions
Rump Steak	Between buttock and sirloin.	An expensive cut with excellent flavour and little waste.	Grilled or fried, traditionally with onions. Châteaubriands should be cut from the rump fillet.
Fillet (or undercut)	Runs beneath the loin bones and under the rump steak.	The most expensive cut with a very delicate texture and not a great deal of flavour.	Usually cut into steaks and grilled, though a whole fillet is sometimes roasted. Is used to make tournedos and *filet mignons*.
Sirloin (including Wing Ribs)	The portion of the back adjoining the rump.	Expensive, but excellent. Sold on the bone, or boned and rolled. Porterhouse steaks are cut from the wing end. T-bone steaks are cut right across the sirloin.	Traditional roasting joint. If cut into steaks, these are fried or grilled.
Fore Ribs	A forwards extension of the wing rib.	A juicy cut, slightly less expensive than sirloin. The flavour is helped by the rather extensive fat. Steaks cut from the fore ribs are sometimes called club steaks.	Can be roasted on the bone, slowly and with a little water in the pan. Boned and rolled makes a tender, well-flavoured pot roast.
Back Ribs (or Short Ribs)	Forwards extension of the fore ribs.	Rather tougher and a little cheaper than fore ribs.	As above.

BEEF (continued)

Cut	Position	Characteristics	Cooking Suggestions
Flat Ribs	Downwards extension of the fore ribs.	Economical rib cut, though rather fat. Is sometimes sold with fore ribs. When de-boned can be used for stewing steak.	May be pot roasted, braised or stewed.
Top Ribs (Together with Back Ribs form Middle Rib)	Downwards extension of the back ribs.	A cheaper cut. These ribs swell in the oven and are sometimes called 'rising ribs' or 'oven busters'.	Can be pot roasted, or roasted very slowly.
Steak meat comprising:			
Leg-of-mutton Cut (or thick top rib)	Between the top ribs and the clod (see below).	A compact, very lean joint usually sold boned.	Requires long, slow cooking and is usually rolled and pot roasted, or salted and boiled. If properly cooked it is very tender.
and			
Chuck and Bladebone (sometimes called shoulder steak)	Thicker top portion of the neck.	First quality braising or stewing steak. Reasonable in price. The meat is improved if the crest muscle at the back of the neck is removed. The roll of the bladebone is sometimes cut into steaks which resemble fillet.	Excellent for braising and stewing. Can be rolled and pot roasted.

BEEF (continued)

Cuts	Position	Characteristics	Cooking Suggestions
Brisket	Lower chest wall.	Very economical joint. Sold with or without bone. If properly cooked, yields good slices of lean meat and excellent dripping.	Usually braised, stewed, or salted and boiled. Can be stewed until tender then finished in a hot oven to simulate roast beef. Is also used, after salting, to make pressed beef.
Forequarter Flank	Muscular wall of the belly.	One of the cheapest cuts. Thicker than, but similar to, thin flank.	May be used for pot roasts and braises. After salting can be boiled or made into pressed beef.
Neck Piece (or Sticking)	The neck of the animal.	A cheap cut, lean in comparison with chuck and bladebone steak. Usually sold as second-grade stewing meat or as mince.	Makes stews and casseroles, and good mince. Is also used for meat pies.
Clod	Front part of the chest.	Cheap cut, similar to neck. A heavy muscle from this part is sometimes removed and sold as 'leg' of beef.	As above.
Skin	Shin portion of the front leg.	Similar to leg, though smaller. Shin meat is sometimes minced.	See leg.

BEEF

BEEF is very nourishing and an excellent source of protein. It offers a great variety of cuts at a wider price range than any other kind of meat.

There is a story that in the eighteenth century the Maréchal de Richelieu offered to all the princes and princesses whom he had taken prisoner during the Hanoverian wars a dinner composed entirely of beef, since he had nothing else at his disposal. The dinner, according to the custom of the times, consisted of soup, four hors-d'œuvres, a 'remove' and six entrées, followed by several other dishes and various sweets—all of them composed of beef. History doesn't say whether the dinner was good!

Some Hints on Buying Beef

The quality of beef depends on:

The *breed* of the animal and the *region* from which it comes. The Aberdeen Angus are the finest beef cattle in these islands. Recently some of the best French beef cattle, the Charolais, have been brought over here for experimental breeding purposes.

The *sex :* the best meat comes from oxen, steers or bullocks, (all names for male animals which have been castrated young), and heifers (females which have not calved). Cow meat, which is lean and rather tough, is sold in large quantities in the North of England and made into excellent pot roasts and stews by experienced north country housewives. It is not so popular in the South. The flesh even of young bulls is lean, tough and rather dark and is, as a rule, only chosen for certain Jewish recipes. (Bull-fighting enthusiasts, however, are delighted to eat the meat of bulls killed in the ring, which is a speciality in certain Spanish taverns on the evening of the fight.)

The *age:* beef from animals between 5 and 6 years old is usually held to have the finest flavour.

The *way in which the animal is fed:* animals which have been pastured in the open and specially raised for beef naturally produce the finest meat.

Care in slaughtering: the meat from beasts which were tired or nervous when they were slaughtered will be tough.

Proper *hanging* of the meat.

No amateur can possibly judge all these factors so, once again, you depend on the butcher to give an honest account of the meat he is selling and to supply a quality which corresponds with the price he asks.

Good quality beef, when it is first cut, is a bright red. Later, when it is exposed to the air, it changes slightly in colour and loses some of its lustre. Tender beef is usually marbled or flecked with fat which should also surround it in a creamy-white layer. (The colour of the fat varies with the breed of the animal and the way in which it has been fed, and the fat of all beef animals tends to be darker at the end of the season when they have been at pasture with no other food but grass.)

The interior of the bones should be rosy and the texture of the beef—and this applies to all meat—should be firm and moist and almost silky to the touch.

Accompaniments to beef. You will find on pages 27–8 all sorts of suggestions for garnishes, most of which go well with beef. Onions, carrots, tomatoes, braised celery or chicory all combine well with the flavour of beef, which is also enhanced by such herbs as thyme, garlic and marjoram. In France it is served with a variety of sauces such as béarnaise, bordelaise, Bercy and so on, though *we* tend to stick to horse-radish.

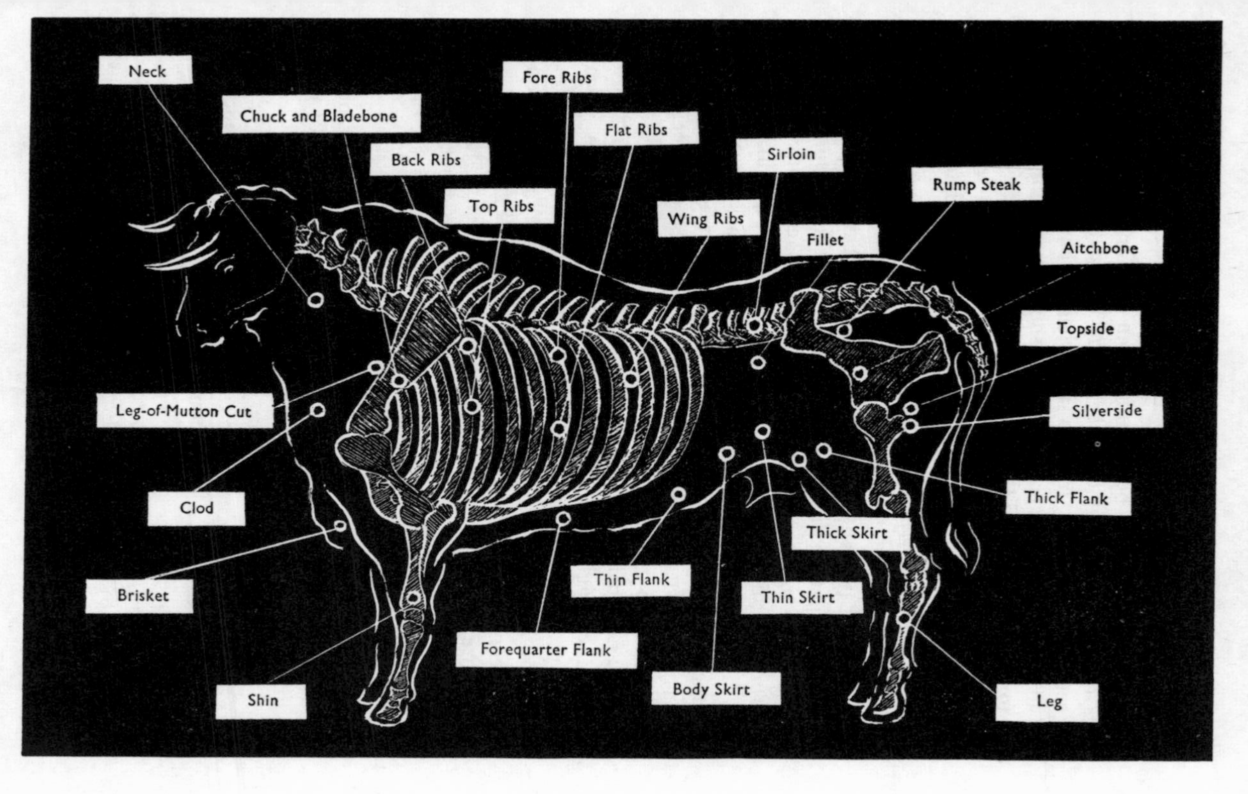

Neck
Chuck and Bladebone
Back Ribs
Top Ribs
Fore Ribs
Flat Ribs
Wing Ribs
Sirloin
Fillet
Rump Steak
Aitchbone
Topside
Silverside
Thick Flank
Leg-of-Mutton Cut
Clod
Brisket
Shin
Forequarter Flank
Thin Flank
Body Skirt
Thin Skirt
Thick Skirt
Leg

Roast Beef

The name 'roast beef' comes from the French 'bœuf rôti'. After the Norman Conquest all the best cuts of meat were eaten by the new masters and their French names were adopted. The coarser cuts—clod, shin, flank, etc., were left for the servants and kept their Saxon names. Roast beef later became a traditional British dish and the word 'rosbif' returned to the French language with a slightly rakish foreign air.

How to choose beef for roasting. The best and most expensive roasts come from the sirloin, which is nowadays often divided into small joints. (If you are fond of undercut it is worth remembering that this does not extend to the thinner end of the sirloin, so to secure the undercut you will have to buy a joint from the thicker end which will weigh at least 4–5 lb.)

The eye of the sirloin, boned and rolled, makes a compact small joint for roasting. Boned joints look attractive and are easy to carve, but they are no more economical than meat on the bone, since the price of the meat per pound is necessarily higher to compensate for the extra labour of boning and for the weight lost. Bone holds the meat firmly in place and prevents the disintegration of the joint at a certain stage in carving. It is also a good conductor of heat, and meat on the bone will cook more evenly, with less loss of gravy.

Fore ribs make a good medium-priced roasting joint but back and top ribs are not so tender and are better pot roasted or braised. If you should decide to try your luck, roast them very slowly with a little water in the pan.

Roasting. Beef, unless it is cooked in a slow oven or wrapped in foil, is inclined to become dry. The French cope with this difficulty by covering the meat with a bard (p. 34).

If you prefer to sear your joint, start it at 445° F (230° C, Gas 8) and lower the heat after a quarter of an hour to 380° F (195° C, Gas 5). Allow about 15 minutes to the lb and 15 minutes over.

Roasting at a moderate temperature gives good results. Pre-heat the oven to 375° F (190° C, Gas 5) and allow about 25 minutes per lb for meat on the bone and about 30 minutes to the lb for boned and rolled joints.

If you are slow roasting at 355° F (180° C, Gas 4) allow from 40–45 minutes per lb.

If you have a large joint and are in a hurry don't try to cook it too fast. It will only harden and shrink. It is better to cut it into slices which can be grilled or sautéd, rather than rush the roasting.

Season beef after it is cooked and leave it to 'rest' for a few minutes with the oven turned off. Deglaze the roasting pan (p. 35) with bouillon, white wine, madeira or sherry according to your taste and what you happen to have on hand, removing any surplus fat before you serve the gravy.

A different way of cooking a rib roast. Add water, little by little, to 1 lb of cooking salt until it is just damp. Cover the meat with a layer of salt a good inch thick.

Put the joint into an oven pre-heated to 380° F (195° C, Gas 5) and cook it for 12 minutes to the pound, allowing 5 minutes extra. The salt will solidify and the meat will keep its full flavour. Be careful to remove all the salt crust before serving.

(If you are roasting ribs in the ordinary way, try covering the lean with a thin bard (p. 34) tied round with string.)

Carving Beef. To carve any meat well it is essential to have a long, thin-bladed knife which is really sharp. Meat is usually carved diagonally across the grain and beef should be sliced thinly. The exception to this is the undercut of the sirloin which should be cut in fairly thick slices with the grain. Where possible, stick the carving fork into the fat to avoid unnecessary loss of gravy from the lean. (In England, where meat is carved at table, this is not as important as in countries where meat is sliced up on a board in the kitchen and then arranged on a dish.)

Beef Steaks

Steaks are cut in various shapes and sizes. The best are from the rump, the fillet and the upper cut of the sirloin. The normal allowance is about 6 oz for each person, though the Americans as a rule allow considerably more. American-type steaks are becoming popular in this country. Ordinary steaks for grilling are generally about 1 inch thick.

Tournedos. A slice of fillet about 1 inch thick, weighing approximately 6 oz. These are exquisitely tender and should be grilled or sautéd very rapidly in '*le temps de tourner le dos*', or just time to turn round.

The long muscle in the bladebone closely resembles the fillet and can be sliced into a very good imitation of a tournedos—in appearance, at least.

Filet Mignon. A small triangular slice of meat weighing not more than 3½ oz cut from the thin end of the fillet. (Slices from the thick muscle in the clod are sometimes sold to the unwary as filet mignon.)

Châteaubriand. Named after the famous French writer whose chef was the 'inventor'. This is a cut from the centre of the fillet about 2 inches thick and weighing at least 12–14 oz. It is usually ordered for two people. Certain restaurants call any thick steak a Châteaubriand.

Entrecôtes should properly be cut from between two wing ribs but they are often taken from the upper part of the sirloin. Fairly tender and rather fat, they have an excellent flavour. Usually they are about ¾-inch thick and one should allow at least 6 oz per person.

Curiously enough the word 'entrecôte', which was originally masculine, has changed its sex and dictionaries now show it as feminine.

Porterhouse Steak. A steak about 1½ inches thick cut from the wing ribs. It corresponds roughly to an entrecôte.

Club Steak. Some butchers describe a steak cut from the fore rib as a club steak. It is rather cheaper than porterhouse.

T-bone Steak. Popular in America and becoming better

known in this country. This is a steak cut right across the fillet end of the sirloin. It weighs from 1½–2 lb, depending upon its thickness and the size of the animal.

Cooking a Steak. Whether they are grilled or sautéd steaks should be cooked with a minimum of fat and 'seized' at a high temperature. Cooking time depends more on thickness than weight. (See the table on p. 38.)

This is an excellent way of cooking a steak:

Take the meat from the refrigerator at least an hour before you want to use it.

Put it in a soup plate with a tablespoon or so of olive oil and, if you like, some thyme, crushed garlic or other herbs. Turn the meat after half an hour.

Have your pan really hot, or the grill glowing, and cook the steak without using any more fat.

Serve it with fresh butter or a sauce, or one of the garnishes on pp. 27–8.

Beef Steaks à l'Italienne Moderately expensive

1 tablespoon olive oil ✦ 4 steaks	Heat the oil to smoking point in a pan. Sauté the beef steaks, turning them once. Keep them hot.
2 tomatoes	Peel the tomatoes, remove the seeds and chop the flesh fairly finely.
1 clove garlic, crushed 1 tablespoon tomato purée	Put the garlic, tomatoes, tomato purée and bouillon into the pan where the steaks were cooked.
2 tablespoons bouillon salt and pepper	Cook gently for 5 or 6 minutes so that the sauce thickens, then season it.
chopped parsley, chervil and oregano	Warm the steaks in the sauce, sprinkle them with the herbs and serve with spaghetti or noodles.

(Oregano, which is a wild form of marjoram, can be bought in tins. When dried, it keeps its flavour well.)

Bœuf Stroganoff Expensive

There are many different versions of Bœuf Stroganoff. This is a good and fairly simple one. Choose juicy steak—fillet if you are feeling extravagant, otherwise buttock steak, or even thick flank if you wish to economize.

The meat should be cut in thin slices diagonally across the grain. It is more easily cut when cold from the refrigerator. Marinade the steak in a little oil for about half an hour before it is cooked.

4 onions ✦ 8–10 mushrooms ✦ 4 tablespoons butter	Chop the onions finely, slice the mushrooms and let them both soften in the melted butter, without colouring.
½ glass white wine ✦ salt and pepper ✦ ½ teaspoon paprika	Add the wine and continue to cook gently for 10–15 minutes with the lid off. Season.
1¼ lb meat	Make an ungreased frying pan very hot. Throw in the meat a few strips at a time and let them brown, shaking the pan. Add the onions and mushrooms. Lower the heat.
1 tablespoon tomato purée salt and pepper	Stir in the tomato purée and season. Cook gently for 10–15 minutes more.
½ glass sour cream 1 teaspoon chopped parsley	Add the cream and let it heat without boiling. Dust with chopped parsley.

(Sour cream, generally called 'cultured cream' is sold by the big dairies and many shops. You can turn ordinary cream sour by adding a little yoghurt and keeping it in a warm place from 3–4 hours.)

Entrecôte Mirabeau Expensive

2 fillets of anchovy 4 tablespoons butter 1 teaspoon lemon juice pepper	Pound the anchovies in a mortar or break them up with a fork. Melt the butter and mix it with the anchovies and lemon. Add pepper but no salt.
1 tablespoon butter 1¼ lb entrecôte ✦ 4–6 fillets of anchovy ✦ pepper and salt ✦ green olives	Brush the steak with melted butter. Grill or sauté it. Season. Spread the anchovy butter over the meat. Garnish it with the fillets and serve surrounded with stoned olives.

Filet de Bœuf en Cocotte Expensive

1 tablespoon fat about 1½ lb fillet steak either larded or barded	Heat the fat to smoking point in a flameproof casserole and brown the meat all over.

1 carrot ✦ 1 onion 1 stick celery ½ glass white wine	Chop the vegetables, arrange them round the meat and let them brown. Add the wine and reduce it to half with the lid off the casserole.
1 small tomato ✦ a bouquet garni	Slice the tomato in half and put it in the casserole, cut-side uppermost. (The steam from the tomato will help to moisten the meat.) Add the bouquet. Cover the casserole and cook on a gentle heat for 20 minutes.
salt and pepper	Season. If the meat has been barded, remove the bard. Strain the sauce and serve.

Steak au Poivre (For two people) Expensive

14 oz Châteaubriand 1 teaspoon peppercorns	Wrap the peppercorns in paper and crush them with a hammer. Rub them into both sides of the meat.
1 tablespoon butter 1 tablespoon oil	Heat butter and oil and boil until they are smoking. Put the steak in the pan, and when moisture beads on the surface turn without piercing. (Lower the heat a little when the meat is 'seized'.)
3 tablespoons brandy	Warm the brandy and pour it flaming over the steak.
salt and pepper	Season.
a pinch cornflour 1 tablespoon butter 2 tablespoons madeira (optional)	Add the cornflour, butter and madeira, scraping the bottom of the pan with a wooden spoon. Stir. Put the meat on to a hot dish, pour the sauce over it and serve.

(White pepper has had the husk removed. Black pepper is spicier and slightly more bitter.)

Tournedos Niçoise Moderately expensive

2 large tomatoes ½ cupful white breadcrumbs ✦ 1 clove garlic, crushed ✦ 1 teaspoon minced parsley ✦ 1 tablespoon olive oil	Cut the tomatoes in half, remove the pips and all the juice you can, by shaking. Mix the breadcrumbs, garlic and parsley. Season, and fill each half tomato, sprinkle with oil and put them for 15 minutes into a moderate oven (355° F, 180° C, gas 4).

4 slices white bread 2 tablespoons olive oil	Cut 4 large round croûtons from the bread, fry them golden-brown in oil and keep them hot.
1 tablespoon butter 4 tournedos ✦ salt and peppers ✦ 4 rolled anchovy fillets	Heat a frying pan, melt the butter and brown the tournedos for a few minutes on each side. Season, and place each one, garnished with an anchovy, on a croûton. Keep hot.
½ glass white wine ✦ 1 tablespoon tomato purée ½ clove crushed garlic 8 stoned green olives	Deglaze the pan with white wine. Add the tomato purée, garlic, sliced olives. Stir well and simmer for 10 minutes or until the sauce is thick.

Pour the sauce over the tournedos and serve with French beans.

BRAISING AND POT ROASTING

Braising is a method of long, gentle cooking, together with vegetables and herbs and a little liquid, in a deep, heavy pan with a tightly-fitting lid. It is really a combination of baking and steaming. Originally glowing coals or *braises* were placed on the concave lid so that heat came from above as well as below—hence the name braising.

Most joints of beef can be braised, though it would be a pity to treat a piece of sirloin or fillet in this way. Braising is an ideal means of turning the leaner and tougher—and consequently cheaper—cuts into tender and appetizing dishes.

It is always wise to make a braise of generous proportions since it will take very little longer to prepare and cook, and is excellent warmed up. The sauce will be smoother if you add a calf's foot and will turn to jelly as it cools. This gives the dish a completely new personality. Braised beef in jelly is delicious.

How to choose meat for braising. The table on pp. 38–42 will give you an idea of the characteristics and relative cost of the various cuts. Chuck, bladebone and back ribs are excellent braised. Flank and brisket, cooked in this way, make an economical dish. The leaner cuts such as topside, silverside and chin require extra fat. This can be supplied by larding or barding (pp. 34 and 35); putting some fresh or salt rind of pork in the bottom of the casserole, or marinading the meat in oil.

Allow for each person 6–8 oz boned meat or 8–12 oz with bone.

To Prepare a Braise. If a braise is to be really tender and succulent (and the best can be cut with a spoon) the lid of the pan must close tightly and the liquid must never boil.

A braise is best cooked in the oven at about 310° F (155° C, Gas 2) surrounded by uniform gentle heat, but it is more economical to cook it very slowly on top of the stove. In this case an asbestos mat beneath the pan helps to spread the heat.

Never braise meat (or deglaze a dish) with water. If you have no stock use bouillon cubes or meat extract. A good brand will heighten the interest of the dish without spoiling the flavour of the meat, but be cautious in adding salt. Whatever the liquid see that it is hot when you add it. If cold, it will harden the meat. (Wine should be either be flambé (see p. 35) or poured gently down the side of the pan.)

Pot Roasting

In its simplest form this consists of 'seizing' a piece of meat in hot fat and then cooking it, with the addition of a little liquid, in a closed pan at a low temperature. This gentle cooking and the action of the imprisoned steam will help to make the meat tender.

A pot roast can be improved by the addition of all sorts of vegetables and herbs, and wine or cider, when it becomes in fact a braise and all the instructions for braising apply.

Steak Braised with Tomatoes Economical

A tough piece of steak prepared in the following way makes an excellent dish

1 tablespoon fat 1–1½ lb meat	Melt the fat in a flameproof casserole and brown the meat all over.
4 tablespoons white wine (optional)	Pour the wine into the casserole and allow it to reduce a little.
3 tablespoons tomato purée ✦ ½ glass bouillon salt and pepper	Stir the tomato purée into warmed bouillon and pour it over the meat. Close the lid and simmer for ¾ hour. Season.
1 teaspoon chopped parsley	Sprinkle with parsley and serve.

Braised Marinaded Beef Expensive

2 tablespoons olive oil 3 tablespoons brandy 3 glasses white wine (or wine mixed with stock) 1 carrot ✦ 2 onions ✦ a stalk of celery ✦ 2 cloves garlic, crushed ✦ a bouquet garni ✦ peppercorns ✦ about 2 lb braising beef	Cut the vegetables in pieces and mix them with the other ingredients together to form a marinade and soak the beef in it for 6 hours, turning from time to time.
a thin slice back pork fat weighing about 6 oz	Lift out the meat and dry it. Secure the bard of pork fat round it with string.
1 tablespoon fat	Heat the fat in a flameproof casserole.
1 onion ✦ 1 carrot a stalk of celery 1 teaspoon chopped parsley 1 crushed clove garlic salt and pepper	Cut the vegetables into dice and brown them lightly. Add the meat and let it brown for at least 5 minutes. Season.
½ glass marinade ✦ 2 teaspoons flour	Sprinkle the flour over the meat and vegetables. Add the marinade little by little, stirring well to avoid lumps. Close the casserole and let it cook very gently for 4 hours. Remove the bard, slice the meat and serve it with the strained sauce from which you have removed all surplus fat.

The wine may be diluted with water and the brandy reduced by half if you wish.

Bœuf Mode (Simple) Moderately expensive

about 2 lb larded topside or top rump 1 tablespoon fat	Make the fat smoking hot in a frying pan and brown the meat all over.
a calf's foot ✦ 6 oz fresh pork rind	Split the calf's foot in two and plunge it into boiling water with the pork rind for a few minutes.
2 tablespoons brandy	Pour the brandy over the meat, let it warm for a moment, and set it alight.
2 shallots ✦ 2 cloves gar-	Put the pork rind, fat side down, into a

lic ✦ salt and pepper ✦ a bouquet garni

flameproof casserole and on top of it the meat, surrounded by the vegetables and the pieces of calf's foot. Close the lid and cook for 10 minutes over a gentle heat, taking care that the rind does not stick.

1 glass white wine
bouillon

Add the wine and then the bouillon, which you have warmed, using enough to come level with the top of the meat. Cover and simmer for 2 hours.

about 10 small onions
4 or 5 carrots ✦ 1 tablespoon fat

Skin the onions and slice the carrots. Brown them in the fat and arrange them round the meat. Simmer another 2 hours. Remove all the surplus fat, the bones from the calf's foot, the bouquet garni and the pork rind. Serve.

Bœuf Mode Mariné Moderately expensive

about 2 lb larded silverside ✦ 2 onions ✦ 1 carrot ✦ 1 stalk of celery ✦ 2 cloves garlic ✦ 1 bay leaf ✦ 2 cloves ✦ 5–6 peppercorns ✦ thyme ✦ 2 tablespoons oil ✦ 1 tablespoon wine vinegar ✦ 3 glasses red wine (diluted with water, if you wish)

Cut the vegetables in large pieces and add the oil and vinegar to make a marinade. Soak the meat in this for 6 hours, turning from time to time. Drain and dry the meat and heat the marinade in a saucepan until it has reduced to about half.

6 oz rind of pork
1 calf's foot

Split the calf's foot and plunge it into boiling water for a few minutes with the pork rind.

1 tablespoon fat ✦ 3 tablespoons brandy

Make the fat very hot in a flameproof casserole and brown the meat. Flamber the meat with brandy and add the calf's foot and pork rind, drained.

salt and pepper

Strain the marinade and add with sufficient bouillon to reach the level of the meat. Season, and simmer 4 hours.

5 or 6 carrots ✦ 8 or 10 small onions ✦ 1 tablespoon fat ✦ a pinch sugar ✦ ½ glass bouillon

Brown the carrots, sliced, and the whole small onions in the fat, add the bouillon and simmer for 1 hour. Adjust the seasoning. Remove the bones from

✦ 1 teaspoon chopped parsley	the calf's foot, the pork rind and any surplus fat, and serve the meat surrounded with vegetables and dusted with parsley.

If you should lard the meat yourself try soaking the lardoons for an hour in a little brandy, or rolling them in garlic crushed with salt and pepper.

Braised Beef with Ginger Economical

1 tablespoon fat 1 onion	Heat the finely chopped onion in fat until it is soft but not coloured, using a flameproof casserole.
about 2 lb top rump or topside	Add the meat and brown it all over.
2 or 3 tomatoes salt and pepper	Skin the tomatoes, remove the pips and cut them in large pieces. Arrange them round the meat.
1 glass of bouillon ½ teaspoon powdered ginger ✦ a stick celery ✦ a bay leaf	Add all these ingredients, adjust the seasoning, cover the casserole and simmer for 3½ hours. Remove the celery, bay leaf and any surplus fat.

Braised Beef with Anchovies Economical

1 rasher lean bacon	Chop the bacon.
1 tablespoon oil ✦ 1 tablespoon butter ✦ about 2 lb braising beef ✦ salt, pepper and nutmeg	Heat the oil and butter in a flameproof casserole and brown the meat. Season, being very cautious with the salt.
4 anchovy fillets ✦ 1 teaspoon minced parsley ✦ 1 glass bouillon	Chop the anchovies and sprinkle them, with the parsley, round the meat. Add the bouillon, cover and simmer for 3½ hours. Remove the surplus fat and serve.

Bœuf Braisé Creole Moderately expensive

about 2 lb chuck, flank, rib or brisket	Make two rows of fairly deep incisions at regular intervals on the upper surface of the meat.
4 oz back pork fat	Cut the fat into lardoons and the olives

8 black olives	in half lengthwise, and insert them alternately with lardoons into the incisions.
1 tablespoon fat	Melt the fat in a flameproof casserole.
1 large onion	Slice the onion and brown with the meat.
4–5 tablespoons rum	Pour the rum over the beef, warm and then light it, spooning it flaming over the meat.
4 tomatoes ✦ 3 crushed cloves garlic ✦ a bouquet garni ✦ 8 peppercorns	Chop the tomatoes after removing skin and pips. Crush the peppercorns and add them with the bouquet and tomato to the meat. Cover the casserole and put it in a low oven. Cook gently for 4 hours. If the sauce becomes too thick add a little warm bouillon. Remove the bouquet and serve.

This dish should be accompanied by rice or noodles.

Bœuf Braisé en Terrine Moderately expensive

about 2 lb braising beef 1 tablespoon fat	Heat the fat in a frying pan and brown the meat all over.
4 tomatoes ✦ 1 onion 1 carrot ✦ a branch of celery ✦ 1 clove garlic 1 teaspoon chopped parsley	Remove the skin and pips from the tomatoes. Chop all the vegetables and put them into a casserole round the meat. Season.
½ glass white wine 2 tablespoons sherry or madeira	Add the wine and sherry, close the casserole, and simmer for 3½–4 hours, opening the lid as little as possible.

Ragoûts and Daubes

A ragoût is, by definition, a dish made with meat, poultry, vegetables or fish cut into even-sized pieces and cooked in a sauce. The nearest English equivalent is a brown stew. Although they are not recommended for people with a delicate digestion, ragoûts can be delicious, varied and economical.

Daubes were originally prepared in *daubières*, deep pans of earthenware or copper which were sealed hermetically with a roll of flour-and-water paste round the edge of a concave lid which held a layer of glowing charcoal. The *daubière* was put in the hot cinders or on a corner of the stove and simmered for twelve hours. This delightful method of cooking is almost impossible nowadays, but the lid can still be sealed with paste or at least be heavy enough not to allow any steam to escape. In any case, you should open the lid as little as possible during cooking.

As in braising the even heat of the oven is preferable to a low heat on top of the stove, though less economical. The oven should be pre-heated to about 445° F (230° C, Gas 8) and lowered to about 355° F (180° C, Gas 4) after a quarter of an hour. Both daubes and ragoûts should be cooked so gently that the liquid just trembles.

How to buy the meat. In France, meat cut in pieces is generally sold under the name of *bourguignon*, while in England it is described as stewing steak. Cheap stewing steak, besides being tough, will contain more waste and possibly some meat which is not fresh.

You can choose a piece of meat and cut it up yourself, or ask the butcher to do this for you.

Most cuts of beef are suitable for ragoûts, though you should avoid those which are too dry or gelatinous. The tables on pp. 38–42 show the characteristics of the different cuts.

Allow 6–8 oz boned meat or 8–12 oz meat with bone for each person.

Preparation. For a daube, meat is usually cut into squares measuring about 2½ inches; for a ragoût, bourguignon or a carbonade, about 2 inches, and for a goulash, about 1½ inches.

For a daube, try larding the meat with strips of back pork fat rolled in a mixture of chopped garlic, minced parsley, salt and pepper.

Never forget that the flavour and texture of these dishes depend on very gentle cooking, otherwise the meat hardens and cannot absorb the fragrance of the sauce. The flavour will also be affected by the quality of the wine or beer which is used.

A ragoût is often better warmed up, so if some should be left there is no problem. It is excellent combined with potatoes or noodles, or gratiné in the oven.

Bourguignon Economical

about 2 lb roll of silverside ✦ 2 tablespoons lard	Heat the lard in a flameproof casserole. Cut the meat into 2-inch squares and brown them all over.
4 oz lean bacon ✦ 8 small onions left whole, or 3 or 4 medium onions, quartered 1 tablespoon flour	Dice the bacon, and brown it with the onions. Dredge with the flour and let this colour too.
1 clove garlic, crushed 2 glasses red wine (optional)	Add the garlic and stir in the wine.
1 tablespoon tomato purée salt and pepper ✦ a bouquet garni ✦ 1 teaspoon minced parsley	Add the tomato purée and the bouquet. Season, and simmer for 3 hours. If the sauce reduces too much dilute it with ½ glass warm bouillon. Remove the surplus fat and the bouquet and serve sprinkled with parsley.

Bourguignon No. 2 Moderately expensive

about 2 lb topside of beef 3 tablespoons brandy	Cut the meat into 2-inch squares and brown it in a frying pan, then put it, drained of fat into a flameproof casserole. Warm the brandy, light it and pour it flaming over the meat.
4 oz green bacon ✦ 1 tablespoon flour	Add the bacon, diced. Sprinkle with flour and let this brown, stirring from time to time.
2 glasses red wine ✦ 1 glass bouillon ✦ a pinch of thyme ✦ a bay leaf ✦ 1 clove crushed garlic ✦ salt and pepper	Add the red wine, stirring all the time, and warm bouillon, parsley, bay leaf, garlic and seasoning. Simmer for 2 hours.
6 or 8 small onions 1 tablespoon fat	Brown the onions in very hot fat, and add them to the meat. Cook very gently for 1 hour more.
1 dessertspoon finely chopped parsley	Remove the bay leaf and the surplus fat and dust with parsley.

A few mushrooms sautéd in butter and added 15 minutes before it is ready will make this dish still better.

Carbonade Flamande Economical

This is a Belgian dish made with beer. As with wine, the

flavour of the dish will be influenced by the quality of the beer, so to make a good carbonade, use a good beer.

2 tablespoons fat 4 onions ✦ about 2 lb top rump ✦ 2 tablespoons flour	Melt the fat in a flameproof casserole and soften the onions. Add the meat, cut in 2-inch squares and brown it with the onions. Sprinkle in the flour, stirring all the time.
1 slice white bread 1 tablespoon French mustard ✦ a bouquet garni salt and pepper	Season the meat, add the bouquet and lay the bread, spread with mustard on both sides, on top of the meat.
about 1 pint beer	Pour in beer level with the top of the meat. Simmer for 3 hours, adding more beer if necessary. Remove the bouquet and serve with boiled potatoes.

Daube Italienne Economical

about 2 lb braising beef 4 oz back pork fat ✦ 1 teaspoon minced parsley 1 clove garlic, crushed salt and pepper	Cut the meat into pieces about 2½ inches square and the pork fat into lardoons, rolling these in garlic, parsley, pepper and salt. Lard each piece of meat.
1 tablespoon fat 1 glass white wine or stock	Brown the meat all over in hot fat, add the warmed wine and cook until it is almost evaporated.
1 carrot ✦ 2 onions 2 sticks celery ✦ 1 dessertspoon finely-chopped parsley	Slice the vegetables finely. Add them to the meat and let them brown for a moment or two adding, if necessary, a little more fat.
3 tablespoons tomato purée ✦ salt and pepper	Add the tomato purée and bouillon to the level of the meat. Season, cover and simmer for 4 hours. Remove unwanted fat.

Goulash

Goulash is an Austro-Hungarian dish, spicy and extremely good. Any remains of this dish will make an excellent soup.

12 onions	Slice the onions in fine rings. Heat the fat in a flameproof casserole and cook the onions until they are transparent.

about 2 lb stewing steak
1 tablespoon lard

Heat the lard to smoking point in a frying pan. Brown the meat, which you have cut into 1½-inch squares. Lift it out and add it to the onions.

1½ tablespoons paprika
1 tablespoon flour
¼ teaspoon cayenne pepper
salt to taste

Dredge the meat with flour, paprika, cayenne pepper and salt. Stir well.

5 tomatoes ✦ 2 tablespoons tomato purée ✦ 2 or 3 cloves of garlic, crushed
1 teaspoon carraway seeds (optional)

Remove skin and pips from the tomatoes and add them to the crushed garlic, tomato purée and carraway seeds.

2 glasses red wine (or stock) ✦ 1 glass bouillon

Pour in the wine and bouillon, warmed. Cover and cook very gently for 2½ hours.

1 lb potatoes

Peel and slice the potatoes. Put them into the casserole, salting lightly. Cook for another ¾ hour. Remove any unwanted fat, and serve.

Goulash Soup

Warm up any remains of goulash with some bouillon. Sharpen the seasoning with paprika and a dash of cayenne pepper. Add some more sliced potatoes and cook for an hour. Goulash soup should be rather thick. Do buy genuine Hungarian paprika: it is worth a hunt to find it.

Beef Casserole Very economical

For this dish you can use either forequarter flank or thick flank (top rump) and fresh flageolets (small kidney beans) or fresh white haricot beans.

a good 2 lb meat ✦ salt and pepper ✦ 1 tablespoon fat

Cut the meat into medium-sized pieces, rub it with pepper and salt, and brown it all over in a large frying pan. Arrange the meat in a fireproof dish.

1 onion ✦ 1 tablespoon flour ✦ 1 teaspoon moist brown sugar ✦ 2 teaspoons vinegar ✦ a bay leaf ✦ 1 glass water

Slice the onion and brown it in the frying pan; sprinkle with flour and sugar. Add the vinegar and bay leaf, stirring all the time, and then the water. Adjust the seasoning. Bring to the boil.

the juice of ½ lemon 1 tablespoon light French mustard	Stir in the lemon juice and mustard and pour the sauce over the meat. Put the dish into an oven pre-heated to 355° F (180° C, gas 5) and cook for 2 hours.
1 lb beans ✦ salt and pepper ✦ 1 tablespoon lemon juice	Plunge the beans, sliced, into boiling salted water. Cook with the lid off until they are tender but firm. Drain, season and sprinkle with lemon juice to preserve their colour. ½ hour before the dish is ready add the beans, mixing them lightly with the gravy.
1 large onion	Choose a mild-flavoured onion. Slice it into rings and use them to garnish the dish.

Ragoût with Artichokes and Peas

Moderately expensive

This is an Italian recipe which is particularly delicate and unusual in flavour. It should be made in spring with fresh vegetables and a tender, juicy piece of meat which does not require long cooking.

3 onions ✦ 1 clove garlic 1 teaspoon chopped parsley ✦ 2 tablespoons olive oil ✦ 2 lb meat	Chop the onions and garlic and let them colour in hot oil in a flameproof casserole. Brown the meat, cut into 2-inch squares, and sprinkle with parsley.
4 small tender artichokes	Remove the outside leaves and trim the rest with scissors. Quarter the artichokes, being very careful to remove the hairy choke.
1 lb new green peas ✦ salt and pepper ✦ a sprig rosemary ✦ 1 teaspoon castor sugar ✦ 1 glass white wine ✦ ½ glass bouillon	Shell the peas and arrange them round the meat with the artichokes. Add herbs and seasoning, the wine and warmed bouillon. Cover and cook gently for 1½ hours.

Pot-au-Feu

Pot-au-feu is a classic French dish which provides meat course, vegetables and soup in one. The ingredients vary according to the region, but the method of preparation is always more or less the same.

You can use lean meat such as silverside which makes excellent broth, or forequarter flank which, even after long cooking, provides quite succulent meat. You will find the characteristics of the various cuts of beef on p. 38. Which you use is largely a matter of personal preference.

The flavour of the broth will be improved if you add chicken giblets, knuckle of veal and beef marrowbone. Cabbage, potatoes, bacon or ham bones will make the broth cloudy, but some ox liver will help to keep it clear. (If you really want to add cabbage, blanch the leaves first in boiling water.) Mutton has too strong a flavour and is rarely used in a pot-au-feu.

The meat will reduce considerably during cooking and 2 lb of fresh meat will only give about 1¼ lb of boiled, so allow at least 7 oz of boned meat or 8½ oz meat with bone for each person.

Preparation. If you are chiefly interested in having a good piece of boiled beef, then put the meat into boiling water and add salt after it is cooked.

If you prefer an excellent broth, put the meat into cold salted water and heat it slowly. As the temperature rises the juices from the meat will be drawn out and yield their flavour to the broth. Never let the liquid boil, just tremble gently. To ensure an even temperature slip an asbestos mat beneath the pan.

To improve the colour of the soup, roast the onions before adding them, or leave on the skins, but make sure that they are not gritty. Browning, which is the lazy way out, adds a slight, unwelcome flavour of its own.

Pot-au-feu must be carefully and repeatedly skimmed until all the grey scum has been removed, or it will look muddy and unattractive.

Before serving, remove some of the fat. Good broth should be sparkling with tiny, bright eyes of fat, and not staring from one great, greasy cyclops eye. It is easier to remove the congealed fat when the soup has cooled.

How to serve pot-au-feu. Both the broth and vegetables are eaten from the same plate as the soup (and don't forget to heat the soup plates). The meat is served in a dish surrounded with boiled potatoes and extra vegetables. Since a great deal of the savour has been lost during cooking, accompany the meal with mustard, pickles, horse-radish sauce or gherkins, and coarse salt.

In some restaurants the broth is served in individual earthenware pots, hence the name *petite marmite*.

Pot-au-feu is very good warmed up, but it is wise to leave the meat in the broth so that it does not dry up. The bouillon should be boiled up each day and should not be kept too long, as the vegetables quickly turn it sour.

In some regions of France a '*soupe perpetuelle*' is kept on the stove all through the year. This is renewed with fresh materials, not cooked scraps like the dubious stock pot so much admired by the Victorians.

A Good Pot-au-Feu Economical

1¼ lb lean beef 1 lb chicken giblets 1 lb bones ✦ coarse salt	Put the meat (the bones chopped small) and the giblets into a heavy saucepan with about 6 pints of cold water. Salt, and bring to the boil. Skim carefully and add a glass of cold water. Skim once more.
2 onions ✦ 2 cloves 3 carrots ✦ 2 turnips ¼ celeriac root ✦ 4 leeks a bouquet garni ✦ 2 cloves garlic ✦ 10 peppercorns	Brown one of the onions in the oven and stick the other with cloves. Cut the carrots, turnips and celeriac into long slices. Tie the white part of the leeks into a bundle.
1 lb forequarter flank of beef	Add the vegetables and the meat and skim once more. Cover the pan, leaving the lid slightly open, and simmer for 4 hours, taking care that the liquid never boils.
a beef marrow bone	Wrap the marrow bone in muslin and add it ½ hour before the pot-au-feu is ready.

The marrow, which has been prevented by the muslin from falling out, is delicious spread on slices of oven-toasted bread and served with the broth.

Variations to the Pot-au-Feu

Pot-au-feu albigeois is made with 1 lb lean beef to 1 lb knuckle of veal and ½ lb raw ham. Besides the usual vegetables, half a cabbage (blanched beforehand) and 6 oz dried haricot beans are used, and a little goose pâté and a dried sausage are added ¾ hour before the end of cooking time.

Poule au pot. The giblets mentioned in the basic pot-au-feu recipe are replaced by a chicken stuffed with sausage meat, raw ham, garlic, onion and the chicken liver.

Languedocienne: a piece of salt streaky pork, previously blanched, is used instead of the giblets.

Potées are thick soups made with salt pork or unsmoked bacon, potatoes and cabbage, and eaten in the same way as pot-au-feu.

Ragoût with Peppers Economical

3 green peppers
2 onions ✦ 2 lb topside or top rump

Remove the seeds and cut the peppers in strips. Slice the onions. Cut the beef in 2-inch squares and put it in a casserole, covered with the vegetables.

12 prunes (optional)
8 small potatoes

Peel the potatoes and arrange them in the casserole with the prunes.

3 tablespoons tomato purée ✦ ½ glass bouillon
salt and pepper ✦ ½ teaspoon caster sugar.

Stir the tomato purée into the bouillon and pour it over the meat. Season, cover and cook in a gentle heat for 3 hours.

NOTE: The prunes should first be soaked for an hour or two in cold water, unless you use the tender Californian kind.

Minced Beef

Mincing is an excellent way of using the cheaper cuts of beef which normally require long, slow cooking. Mince can be rapidly prepared in a number of different ways. Besides the recipes which follow you will find some ideas in the chapter on Remains of Cold Meat, p. 191.

How to buy mince. The cheapest mince comes mostly from the neck and shin whilst the most expensive, which is passed through a finer grid, is made of trimmings from the better cuts. This is often described as Hamburger steak. Unless you are confident that your butcher is using only fresh and clean meat you may prefer to choose your own cut and mince it at home.

Mince made from the tougher and leaner cuts like shin has an excellent flavour, and with the addition of a little sausage meat it gains in richness and texture.

Allow about 5 oz for each person unless you are adding breadcrumbs, flour, etc., when 4 oz will be sufficient.

Keeping minced meat. Mince does not keep well and should be eaten as soon as possible after it is bought.

Some ways of preparing minced meat. There are many ways of using minced meat besides the familiar cottage pie, *bolognese* sauce for spaghetti, or the Hamburger. The following list can be used as a reminder, while the recipes which follow give some more unusual ideas:

Meat balls: round balls made of minced meat with all sorts of additions, sautéd and finished in a covered pan with sauce.

Meat cakes similar, but flatter in shape.

Croquettes. Though some purists insist that croquettes should consist of cooked meat, fish, game, etc., flaked and mixed with thick sauce and then egg-and-breadcrumbed and fried in deep fat, we use this word to describe minced meat mixed with chopped mushrooms or ham and formed into small sausage-shaped rolls which are then fried.

Meat loaf: minced meat mixed with various ingredients and shaped into a round or oblong loaf.

Mince: mince can be prepared and served in a casserole on toast, shaped in a mould, or browned in a fireproof dish.

Stuffing. Minced meat forms the basis of many stuffings for vegetables, fish and so on.

The use of bread with minced meat

In many recipes minced meat is mixed with bread, which is one reason why such dishes are economical. The proportions vary, but be sure that your meat loaf doesn't become a glorified bread pudding!

If possible, use stale bread. Cut off the crusts and soak the crumb for a few minutes in milk, bouillon or water, according to the recipe. Squeeze the bread as dry as possible and crumble it with your fingers—and if, as we hope, you have just washed your hands, be sure they carry no taint of soap or detergent.

Incidentally, the best way of mixing meat balls is with your hands; as the various ingredients must be well worked together.

Steak Tartare Expensive

This dish is usually prepared at table and is quite amusing for those who enjoy audience participation in their cooking.

Choose tender steak, either rump or fillet. It will taste better if it is freshly minced or scraped at home. You will need from 1 to 4 yolks of egg, the number being a matter of personal taste and best decided by experiment.

Since raw meat does not look particularly attractive and you will be closely watched by your guests (unless you decide to break with tradition and carry out the whole operation in the kitchen) it is important to present your materials as attractively as possible.

Pile the steak in the middle of your prettiest dish and surround it with mounds of capers, finely-chopped onion and parsley. Break the eggs carefully and set each yolk, in its half shell, in the meat. Be sure that all you need is ready on the table, including a deep dish in which to stir the oil and vinegar mixture. This must be large enough to hold the steak as well.

4 yolks of egg ✦ 4 tablespoons olive oil ✦ 1 tablespoon Worcestershire sauce ✦ 1 tablespoon vinegar ✦ 2 tablespoons French mustard ✦ salt and pepper

Stir all these ingredients together in a deep dish to make a piquant sauce.

1 lb minced steak 1 finely-chopped onion 2 teaspoons minced parsley ✦ 2 teaspoons capers	Mix the steak, onions, parsley, capers and the sauce, stirring lightly with a fork.

Steak tartare is very good accompanied by a tossed green salad.

Russian Steaks Economical

1 egg ✦ 1¼ lb minced beef 1 tablespoon butter ✦ 1 teaspoon chopped parsley salt and pepper	Beat the egg and soften the butter. Mix all the ingredients and form them into 4 rather thick steaks.
4 tablespoons flour 1 egg ✦ 1 teaspoon water breadcrumbs	Dip the steaks in flour; then beaten egg diluted with water, and lastly plenty of breadcrumbs.
3 tablespoons butter 1 tablespoon oil	Make the butter and oil smoking hot and fry the steaks 3 minutes on each side. Serve with fried parsley.*

* To fry parsley, plunge it into a smoking-hot deep-frying pan. When the parsley comes to the surface lift it out, and drain it on soft kitchen paper.

Andalusian Steaks Moderately expensive

1 or 2 onions ✦ 1 tablespoon butter ✦ 1 clove garlic, crushed	Chop the onions finely and soften them in butter. Add the garlic and cook a moment more.
1¼ lb minced meat ✦ 1 egg salt and pepper ✦ 1 teaspoon minced parsley	Work the onion mixture, meat, egg and seasoning together in a bowl and form into 4 steaks.
1 tablespoon flour	Coat the steaks with flour.
2 large tomatoes ✦ 2 tablespoons olive oil	Cut the tomatoes in two and shake them to remove some of the seeds. Season, and fry them in hot oil. Lift them on to a hot dish.
1 tablespoon butter ✦ ½ teaspoon cornflour mixed with 1 teaspoon butter to form a roux ✦ 3 or 4 tablespoons sherry, madeira or white wine	Heat the butter in the same pan and fry the steaks for about 4 minutes on each side. Put a half tomato on top of each and keep warm on a dish. Reduce the heat. Mix the roux and wine in the pan and bring to the boil, scraping the pan well. Pour the sauce over the meat.

Garnish the dish with a few leaves of lettuce or watercress, black olives and a twist of lemon peel on top of each steak.

Hamburger Steaks with Bacon Economical

1¼ lb minced beef ✦ 1 egg
3 tablespoons tomato purée
salt and pepper

Mix all the ingredients and form 16 small, flat steaks of equal size.

2 or 3 onions ✦ 1 tablespoon oil or fat ✦ 8 rashers bacon

Slice the onions and fry them in oil or fat. Sandwich a layer of onion between every pair of steaks and wrap each in a rasher of bacon secured with a wooden toothpick.

1 tablespoon butter

Sauté the hamburgers for 5 minutes on each side, or cook them in a fairly hot oven (400° F, 200° C, Gas 6) for 15 minutes, turning them once.

Meat Balls Very economical

2 tablespoons fat ✦ 2 or 3 onions

Chop the onions finely and let them soften, but not colour, in hot fat.

1 egg ✦ salt and pepper

Beat the egg lightly in a large bowl. Season.

2 or 3 slices bread
bouillon ✦ 1¼ lb mince (or 1 lb minced meat and 4 oz. sausage meat) ✦ 1 teaspoon chopped parsley

Soak the bread in bouillon, squeeze it as dry as possible, crumble and mix it with the egg, onions, meat and parsley. Make 8 meat balls.

2 tablespoons flour
2 tablespoons fat

Roll the meat balls in flour and fry them in smoking-hot fat until they are golden-brown all over. Serve with tomato sauce or sauce chasseur.

Dutch Meat Balls Economical

These meat balls should be prepared and left overnight in a cool place to absorb the flavour of the sauce. Next day, warm them up for 15 minutes and add the cream just before serving with potato purée or noodles.

1 large onion ✦ 3 tablespoons breadcrumbs ✦ 4 oz sausage meat ✦ 1 lb minced

Grate the onion into a large bowl. Work well together with the breadcrumbs, meat, egg and seasoning.

beef ✦ 1 egg ✦ salt and pepper 3 tablespoons tomato purée ✦ 2 glasses bouillon	Form 8 meat balls and put them into a fireproof casserole. Mix the tomato purée and bouillon, and pour them over the meat balls. Close the casserole and cook very gently, in the oven or on top of the stove for 1½ hours. Keep overnight. Next day, heat the dish through.
a small jar sour cream.*	Add the sour cream just before serving, being very careful that the sauce does not boil afterwards.

* Sour, or 'cultured', cream is now sold by the big dairies and many delicatessen stores.

Viennese Meat Cakes Economical

This is an excellent recipe. Be sure that the bread is finely crumbled and the potatoes well sieved.

Since the anchovies are salt, be cautious with your seasoning. The flavour of anchovy tends to disappear during cooking but it adds interest to the sauce.

2 slices bread ✦ bouillon 1 lb minced beef ✦ 4 oz sausage meat ✦ 1 teaspoon butter ✦ 1 teaspoon grated lemon rind ✦ 2 yolks egg 2 or 3 freshly cooked potatoes ✦ salt, pepper and nutmeg	Soak, squeeze and crumble the bread. Sieve the potatoes and work everything well together with your finger tips.
2 egg whites	Whip the egg whites and fold them into the mixture. Form 8 meat cakes, and let them stand for ½ hour.
2 tablespoons butter ✦ 2 shallots ✦ 3 tablespoons chopped fresh herbs (principally chives, if possible) 2 fillets anchovy ✦ the juice of ½ lemon ✦ 4 tablespoons white wine ✦ pepper	Mince the shallots. Melt the butter in a frying pan and soften the herbs and shallots for a few minutes. Raise the heat and brown the meat cakes all over. Crush the anchovies with a fork and distribute them round the meat. Stir in the wine and lemon juice. Cover and simmer gently for 20 minutes, turning the meat cakes after 10 minutes. Adjust the seasoning. Strain the sauce and serve.

Dolmas Very economical

Dolmas, which come from Greece and Turkey, should be made with vine leaves and mutton. However, the leaves of cabbage, spinach beet, Cos lettuce, or even large spinach leaves make successful substitutes. You can also use beef instead of mutton. Dolmas offer a pleasant way of eating cabbage when other vegetables are scarce. They appear difficult to prepare but are really quite simple.

1 cabbage (or the other leaves mentioned)	Blanch the cabbage in boiling water for 3 minutes, drain and cool.
2 onions ✦ 1 tablespoon butter	Chop the onions finely and soften them in butter.
1 lb minced meat ✦ 1 egg ✦ 1½ cups cooked rice ✦ a pinch cinnamon ✦ 2 tablespoons tomato purée ✦ salt and pepper ✦ chopped parsley and other herbs	Mix all together and divide into 8 portions. Place each in the middle of a leaf (removing the coarsest part of the stalk and overlapping several smaller leaves if necessary). Allow a good margin of leaf beyond the stuffing and roll each dolmas, firming it by wringing gently in the corner of a clean cloth.
1 tablespoon lard ✦ 2 glasses bouillon ✦ salt and pepper	Melt the lard in the bottom of a flameproof casserole, brown the dolmas, add the bouillon, and put an inverted plate on top of them to hold them in position. Close the lid of the casserole and cook very gently for an hour. Put the dolmas in a hot dish over boiling water, or in a warm oven, while you make the sauce.
1 yolk egg ✦ the juice 1 lemon	Put the egg and lemon juice into a bowl and add the liquid from the casserole drop by drop beating all the time. Pour over the dolmas and serve with a twist of lemon peel.

Dolmas should be highly seasoned. One can add a good teaspoon of paprika and a pinch of cayenne pepper to the mixture and put some diced bacon into the casserole to brown with the dolmas. They are very good cold.

Rice and Meat Balls Very economical

Served with vegetables these rice and meat balls make a very satisfying meal.

3 slices of bread ✦ milk to moisten the bread ✦ 1 cup cooked rice ✦ 1 lb minced beef ✦ 1 tablespoon melted butter ✦ 5 tablespoons grated parmesan cheese salt and pepper	Soak, squeeze and crumble the bread. Add the rice, meat, butter and cheese. Season, and form 8 firm balls.
2 tablespoons flour ✦ 1 egg 1 teaspoon water ✦ 1 teaspoon oil ✦ 3 tablespoons breadcrumbs	Rolls the balls in flour. Dip them in beaten egg, water and oil, and then in breadcrumbs.
½ cup oil	Fry the balls in smoking-hot oil for 10–15 minutes, turning them carefully.

This recipe can be varied by soaking the bread in bouillon instead of milk, deep-frying the balls and serving with tomato sauce (p. 203).

Meat Loaves

You can improve the flavour of a meat loaf by adding minced veal to the beef, and give it a richer texture with the addition of a little sausage meat.

Meat loaves are as good cold as hot. If you are cooking for a picnic wrap the loaf in foil before baking it in the oven. It will remain compact in shape, rich in flavour and will be easy to carry and cut. The inside will be pink instead of brown.

Baked Meat Loaf (Cold or hot) Very economical

1 onion ✦ 1 teaspoon fat 3 slices of bread ✦ ½ glass bouillon	Chop the onion very finely and let it soften in hot fat. Soak, squeeze and crumble the bread.
1 egg ✦ 6 oz sausage meat 1 lb minced beef ✦ 1 teaspoon chopped parsley salt and pepper	Mix onion, bread, egg, meat, parsley and seasoning. Make a sausage-shaped loaf.
4 oz caul fat	Plunge the caul fat into boiling water to

soften it. Spread it on the table. Wrap up the loaf and tie with string.

3 tablespoons oil or fat
thyme or rosemary

Put the meat loaf in a fireproof dish. Brush it with oil or melted fat and sprinkle with herbs. Let it brown for 10 minutes in an oven pre-heated to 445° F (230° C, Gas 8). Reduce the heat to 355° F (170° C, Gas 3) and bake for 40 minutes.

Viennese Meat Loaf Economical

2 slices bread ✦ ½ cup bouillon ✦ 1 onion ✦ 1 clove garlic ✦ 1 lb minced beef ✦ 6 oz sausage meat
salt and pepper

Soak the bread in bouillon, squeeze it dry and crumble it into a bowl. Chop the onion and garlic finely, mix with the meat, season and work together with the bread to form a meat loaf.

2 tablespoons flour ✦ 4 rashers bacon ✦ 1 onion sliced in rings ✦ 1 lemon
3 tablespoons grated parmesan (optional)

Roll the loaf in flour, put it in a fireproof dish covered with bacon, onion rings and some thin slices of lemon. Sprinkle with parmesan cheese if you wish.

2 tomatoes ✦ 1 onion
1 carrot ✦ a stick celery
3 tablespoons cream ✦ 1 tablespoon oil ✦ a bay leaf
½ glass bouillon

Peel the tomatoes and remove the pips. Chop all the vegetables and mix with the cream, oil and bay leaf, and arrange them round the edge of the dish. Bake in a hot oven (445° F, 230° C, Gas 8) for 15 minutes. Reduce the heat to 355° F, (170° C, Gas 3) and cook for 1¼ hours, basting every 10 minutes, adding bouillon a little at a time.

½ teaspoon arrowroot

If the sauce requires thickening, mix the arrowroot with a little cold water and stir it into the sauce 5 minutes before the dish is ready. Remove the bay leaf and serve.

Minced Meat Mould Very economical

1 tablespoon butter ✦ 1 tablespoon flour ✦ 3 tablespoons tomato purée ✦ 1 cup bouillon

Melt the butter in a saucepan, add the flour and then the tomato purée, stirring all the time. Mix in the bouillon, a little at a time, being careful to avoid lumps. Cook gently for 5 minutes.

1¼ lb minced beef ✦ salt and pepper ✦ ½ clove garlic, crushed ✦ 1 teaspoon minced parsley	Add the meat, garlic, parsley and seasoning and cook together for a few minutes. Cool.
2 eggs	Beat the eggs and add them to the mince. Pour the mixture into a buttered mould, stand it in a tin of boiling water and cook in a moderate oven (355° F, 180° C, Gas 4) for ¾ hour.

Turn out on to a dish and cover the meat with tomato or chasseur sauce (p. 200). If you have used a ring mould, fill the centre with cauliflower and surround it with boiled potatoes and whole braised onions.

Cuban Mince Very economical

1 cup rice ✦ 2 or 3 green peppers	Throw the rice into boiling salted water. Cook for 5 minutes with the lid off. Drain. Cut the peppers in fine slices after removing the seeds.
3 tablespoons olive oil 1 lb minced beef ✦ salt and pepper	Heat the oil in a frying pan and brown the peppers. Add the meat and let it colour. Season.
2 eggs ✦ 4 tomatoes	Beat the eggs, draw the pan from the fire and add them to the meat. Skin and slice the tomatoes after removing the pips. Arrange in a buttered fireproof dish alternate layers of tomato, rice, meat, and so on.
2 tablespoons bouillon 2 tablespoons breadcrumbs 3 tablespoons melted butter	Pour the bouillon over the contents of the dish and sprinkle with breadcrumbs and melted butter. Bake in a moderate oven (355° F, 170° C. Gas 3) for ½ hour.

Use up the crust as well as the crumb

Instead of making breadcrumbs from slices of bread and wasting the crusts, try cutting off the whole end of a loaf and scooping out the crumb, leaving a hollow shell to hold a pudding. Prepare it like this:

3½ oz butter or margarine	Melt the butter and trickle it into the hollow crust so that it is buttered all over. Put it in a small greased fireproof dish.
2 or 3 apples ✦ a handful raisins ✦ 1 tablespoon gooseberry jelly ✦ 3 tablespoons caster sugar	Peel the apples and slice them finely. Fill the buttered crust with apple, raisins and gooseberry jelly and sprinkle it with sugar. Bake this for ½ hour.

Paupiettes

Paupiettes are made by rolling slices of beef or veal, rectangular and fairly thin, round a stuffing.

How to choose the meat. Buy very thin slices of tender lean beef—rump steak is quite suitable—cut on the bias to avoid tearing when they are rolled. Allow not more than 3½ oz for each person.

How to prepare paupiettes. The meat, when it is laid out on a flat surface and gently pressed, should be only about one-eighth of an inch think. Put a spoonful or two of stuffing on each slice and roll, wrapping it with a thin slice of bacon if you wish. Tie each paupiette with thread or secure it with a wooden tooth pick.

Cook the paupiettes very slowly so that they become impregnated with the fragrance of the stuffing.

Paupiettes à la Provençale Moderately expensive

4 slices lean beef ✦ 4 oz salt pork ✦ 2 cloves garlic, crushed ✦ 1 teaspoon minced parsley ✦ salt and pepper ✦ 4 rashers fat bacon	Flatten the meat carefully. Chop the salt pork, mix with the other ingredients and season. Divide the stuffing in four and spread it on the slices of beef. Roll, and wrap each slice in bacon. Tie with string.
2 carrots ✦ 3 onions ✦ 1 tablespoon fat ✦ ½ glass white wine	Heat the fat in a flameproof casserole and brown the paupiettes. Slice the onions and carrots and brown them too. Pour in the white wine and let it reduce almost completely.

½ glass bouillon ✦ a bouquet garni ✦ salt and pepper	Add the bouillon and the bouquet garni. Season and cover. Cook for an hour on a very low fire. (If you prefer, you can remove the bacon wrapping and brown the paupiettes in the oven moistened with their own sauce.)
1 teaspoon butter ✦ ½ teaspoon cornflour	Mix the butter and cornflour and stir them into the sauce in the casserole, after removing the bouquet garni. When the sauce has thickened, pour it over the paupiettes and serve.

Les Oiseaux Sans Tête à la Flamande Moderately expensive

4 slices lean beef ✦ pepper 3½ oz salt pork ✦ 4 rashers fat bacon	Flatten the meat and sprinkle it with pepper. Cut the salt pork in 4 pieces and roll up in a slice of beef, wrapping each in a rasher of fat bacon.
1 tablespoon fat ✦ 2 onions 1 teaspoon flour	Melt the fat in a flameproof casserole. Chop the onions and soften them in the fat. Add the paupiettes and let them brown, sprinkled with flour.
1 glass beer ✦ salt and pepper ✦ 1 slice bread light French mustard	Pour in the beer. Season. Spread the bread with mustard and lay it on the paupiettes. Cover the casserole and cook on a very low fire for 2 hours. Remove surplus fat and serve.

Paupiettes à la Creme Expensive

The mixture of meat and anchovies, which seems strange, is really very good. This dish is best served with spinach and potato purée.

6 or 8 fillets of anchovy ½ teaspoon parsley ✦ a small onion ✦ 1 or 2 cloves garlic	Chop the anchovies and herbs finely and mix them together.
4 slices lean beef pepper	Flatten the meat carefully. Pepper it and spread each slice with the mixture you have just prepared. Roll and tie the paupiettes.
2 tablespoons butter	Brown the paupiettes in hot butter.

2 glasses bouillon ✦ a dash of cayenne pepper

Moisten them with bouillon. Season, salting with caution. Cook with the lid off in a very cool oven (310° F, 155° C, Gas 1) for 1 hour.

5 oz fresh cream ✦ a slice of lemon ✦ 1 teaspoon each minced parsley and chives

Add the cream just before serving, heating the sauce without allowing it to boil. Sprinkle with a few drops of lemon juice and the chopped herbs.

USUAL CUTS OF VEAL IN LONDON AND THE HOME COUNTIES

Cut	Position	Characteristics	Cooking Suggestions
Fillet	Upper part of back	Very expensive cut but with minimum waste. Used for escalopes, and schnitzels (cut across the grain).	If roasted, extra fat must be added, either by means of larding, a rich stuffing, or the addition of bacon rolls.
Knuckle	Lower part of hind and fore leg.	Very cheap. The fore knuckle is more tender than the hind, but the bone of the hind knuckle has more marrow content. Knuckle, together with scrag and middle neck, provide stewing and pie veal.	Makes sautés, ragoûts and blanquettes. The bones are useful for broth, and the feet for enriching large braises or making calf's-foot jelly.
Loin	Corresponds to sirloin.	Sold as a joint or divided into chops which may contain kidney. Some butchers sell loin rolled and stuffed.	Used for roasts, sautés and braises. Chops may be grilled or fried.
Best End of Neck	Ribs adjoining loin.	Usually similar in price to loin. Can be divided into cutlets.	May be roasted, or braised. Cutlets are usually fried or sautéd.

VEAL (continued)

Cut	Position	Characteristics	Cooking Suggestions
Middle Neck and Scrag	Base of neck beneath shoulder, and neck	Sold together or separately. Used for pie veal and stewing meat.	Best parts can be braised in one piece; otherwise stewed or used for pies, broth, etc.
Shoulder	Front leg and shoulder.	Cheapest of the roasting joints. The knuckle is sometimes removed leaving the best part, or oyster.	Can be roasted on the bone, or stuffed and rolled. The oyster makes excellent blanquettes, ragoûts and braises.
Breast	As in lamb, the underneath of the body.	A very economical cut which, when stuffed, makes a tasty roast.	Needs long, slow cooking. Besides being stuffed and roasted it can be braised or stewed.

VEAL

VEAL is no more digestible than beef and less nourishing. It is also, if of good quality, more expensive. The finest veal comes from calves of four to six months' old weighing between 120 and 140 lb which have been specially bred and 'managed' to produce the best meat. This is mostly imported from Holland, though an effort is now being made to produce quality veal in this country.

In France they are now using surplus dairy products for the large-scale rearing of the fortnight-old male 'bobby calves' which are otherwise taken from their mothers and slaughtered to produce very low-grade veal. These artificially fed calves are called *pouponettes* after bottle-fed babies.

In Mediterranean countries veal is often greyish-brown because some calves are slaughtered when they are as much as three years old. The Italians call the tender young veal *vitello* and the teenage variety *vitellone.*

Buying veal. The lean of veal should be palest pink and the fat firm, pale and not too sparse. The bones should be tender and translucent. The flesh of a 'bobby calf' is yellowish, flabby, gelatinous and totally lacking in fat. As a calf gets older the flesh becomes darker and the fat yellow.

Allow 6–8 oz per person for boned veal and about 12 oz with bone. If the proportion of bone to meat is very high you may need as much as 1 lb for each person.

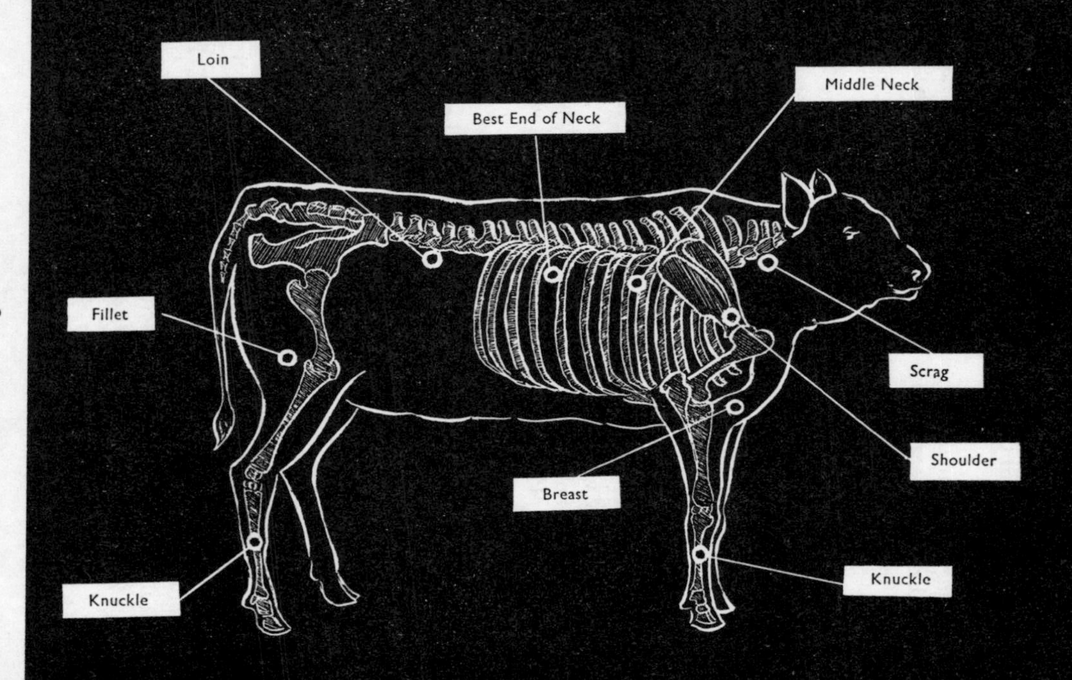
Loin
Best End of Neck
Middle Neck
Fillet
Scrag
Shoulder
Breast
Knuckle
Knuckle

When you buy a joint of veal ask your butcher for some bones to make stock.

Roasts and Braises

As veal is rather dry it is, on the whole, better suited to braising than roasting, though a moist, rather fat stuffing and careful basting will do a great deal to improve a roast.

Roasting. Veal should not be underdone. Unlike red meat, it should never be seared at a high temperature but cooked at about 380° F (195° C, Gas 3) for 40 minutes to the lb.

Veal Stock. To make veal stock put some bones and half a calf's foot, a carrot, onion, stalk of celery, salt and pepper into 3½ pints of water. Simmer for at least 2 hours then add a bouquet of fresh tarragon, or some rosemary and thyme (thyme goes particularly well with veal) and continue to simmer gently for 15 minutes. This stock, if used for basting, will help the meat to keep its flavour. You can replace the calf's foot by a piece of fresh or salt rind of pork but this will not form a jelly when the stock is cold.

If you have no time to prepare stock, use a chicken bouillon cube instead. The delicate flavour and pale colour of the chicken broth go very well with veal.

Braising. The notes on braising in the chapter on beef (p. 43) apply to veal. Most cuts of veal can be used for this purpose. Boned breast and shoulder make delicious and particularly economical braises.

How to serve veal. Veal should be carved in fairly thin slices and this is easy with fillet (the upper part of the leg and not to be confused with the fillet in beef) or the rump end of the loin, but neck, shoulder and any rolled and stuffed joints tend to fall apart and look much less presentable.

Veal goes well with spinach, sorrel, early vegetables, tomatoes, mushrooms and *noisette* potatoes.

Casserole of Veal Moderately expensive

4 oz back pork fat ✦ 2 onions ✦ 1 carrot ✦ a bouquet garni ✦ salt and pepper ✦ about 1½ lb veal	Lay the pork fat in the bottom of a flameproof casserole. Cover it with the sliced vegetables and the herbs, and season. Put the meat on top and cook it for 15 minutes over moderate heat with the lid on.
1 glass dry white wine	Take off the lid, pour the wine gently down the sides of the casserole and let it reduce for a time with the lid off.
Stock ✦ salt and freshly-milled pepper	Pour in stock to the same depth as the meat. Season, cover and cook over very low heat for 1 hour, basting the top of the meat from time to time. Put the meat in a fireproof dish, moisten it with a tablespoon of the liquid, and brown for 10 minutes in an oven pre-heated to 425° F, (220° C, Gas 7). Meanwhile strain the liquid, remove the grease, and let it reduce still further so that it makes a sauce to accompany the veal.

Serve with a purée of sorrel or spinach into which you can stir part of the fat removed from the liquid in which the veal has cooked.

Veal Braised with Ham Moderately expensive

about 1½ lb veal ✦ 1 tablespoon oil ✦ 2 thick slices ham ✦ 2 onions ✦ 1 tablespoon flour	Heat the oil in a flameproof casserole and brown the meat all over. Chop the ham and onions and arrange them round the veal. Dredge with flour.
2 tomatoes ✦ salt and pepper ✦ a bouquet garni	After removing the skin and pips from the tomatoes add them, with seasoning and bouquet garni, to the vegetables in the casserole.
1 glass stock or bouillon	Pour in the stock and cook over a low fire for 1½ hours.
½ cup dried mushrooms soaked for 1 hour in cold water	Drain the mushrooms, add them to the meat and cook for another ½ hour. Remove the surplus fat (which you can mix with spinach purée) and serve with fried croûtons.

Veal with Tomatoes Moderately expensive

about 1½ lb veal ✦ 2 cloves garlic ✦ 4 oz diced bacon 1 teaspoon oil or fat	Cut each clove of garlic in four lengthwise and insert the pieces into 8 slits in the meat. Heat the oil in a flameproof casserole and brown the bacon. Brown the meat too.
4 tomatoes	Cut the tomatoes in half and shake out the seeds. Place them round the meat cut side up.*
1 clove garlic ✦ 2 shallots salt and pepper	Sprinkle the garlic and shallots, finely chopped, over the tomatoes and season.
½ glass white wine or water	Pour the wine down the side of the casserole. Close the lid and cook on a low fire for 1½ hours. When the meat is done lift it out. Crush the tomatoes with a fork and remove the skins. Slice the meat and cover it with sauce.
1 teaspoon chopped parsley	Sprinkle with parsley.

* The tomatoes cook in their skins and add their flavour to the meat without making the sauce too liquid.

Shoulder of Veal with Herbs Economical

This dish can be served hot one day and cold, with its jelly, the next. It should make two meals for four people.

3 lb shoulder of veal (boned) ✦ 3 cloves garlic salt and pepper ✦ 3 teaspoons chopped thyme and rosemary, or fresh tarragon	Flatten the veal, rub it with crushed garlic, salt and pepper, and sprinkle with herbs.
2 tablespoon fat	Heat the fat in a frying pan. Brown the meat all over, drain off the fat and put the meat into a flameproof casserole.
juice of ½ lemon ✦ 2 glasses veal stock	Moisten with the lemon juice and stock. Cover with a heavy, tight-fitting lid and cook on a low fire for 2 hours, turning the meat from time to time.

Serve the meat sliced and covered with its sauce. Put the rest of the slices in a deep dish and cover with the remainder of the strained liquid from the casserole. Put it in a cool place overnight to form a jelly, and serve garnished with parsley and slices of lemon.

Veal Stuffed with Kidney Expensive

This dish should be made with loin rolled and tied round the kidney. It is more economical however if you use boned shoulder or breast. The kidney should be surrounded with its own fat and this, melting inside the meat, gives the dish its special rich and delicate flavour.

Cooked in the oven:

1½ lb meat ✦ salt and pepper ✦ 3 tablespoons butter ✦ 3 tablespoons fresh cream	Rub the meat with salt and pepper. Put it in a fireproof dish and drench it with melted butter and cream.
2 tablespoons stock or water	Roast the meat in a moderate oven (355° F, 180° C, Gas 4) for 1 hour. At the end of the first 15 minutes put the heated stock or water in the pan. Turn the meat half-way through cooking and add some more liquid if necessary.

Cooked on the stove:

2 tablespoons fat ✦ 1½ lb meat ✦ 2 carrots ✦ 2 onions 3½ oz diced bacon ✦ 1 tablespoon flour ½ glass white wine ✦ 1 glass stock ✦ salt and pepper	Using a flameproof casserole, brown the meat in hot fat. Surround the meat with diced vegetables and bacon, sprinkle with flour and let them colour. Trickle in the wine and warm stock, stirring to avoid lumps. Season. Cover and cook over a slow fire for 45 minutes to the lb, adding more liquid if necessary.
2 tablespoons cream (optional)	Skim off the surplus fat and add the cream just before serving.

Ossi Bucchi Bolognese Moderately expensive

4 two-inch slices hind knuckle of veal (containing marrow) ✦ 2 tablespoons oil ✦ 1 tablespoon flour	Season the pieces of meat and flour them lightly. Brown all over.

2 or 3 onions ✦ 2 cloves garlic ✦ 1 glass white wine 4 tomatoes ✦ 3 tablespoons tomato purée ✦ salt and pepper ✦ ½ glass hot water

Add the sliced onions and chopped garlic. Pour in the wine and let it reduce. Remove skin and pips from the tomatoes and add them, quartered, together with the tomato purée, bouquet garni and water. Season. Cover and simmer for 1½ hours, adding water if necessary.

Serve the *ossi buchi* with rice or *pasta* and grated parmesan cheese. The French sometimes prepare *tendrons de veau* (the meat between the ends of the ribs which is sold here as part of the breast) according to this recipe. If you can induce your butcher to provide this particular cut, it makes an economical dish.

Knuckle of Veal with Vegetables Economical

4 oz rind of pork ✦ 2 onions 2 carrots ✦ 3 stalks celery 1 clove garlic a pinch each chopped thyme and rosemary ✦ a bay leaf ✦ grated rind of 1 orange ✦ 4 pieces of knuckle of veal ✦ salt and pepper

Place the rind of pork in the bottom of a flameproof casserole and cover with coarsely chopped vegetables. Sprinkle with herbs and grated orange rind and place the meat on top. Season. Close the lid and cook over a gentle fire for 15 minutes.

½ glass white wine *or* 3 tablespoons madeira ✦ 1 teaspoon flour

Add the wine and let it reduce over the fire. Dust in the flour.

2 tomatoes ✦ 3 tablespoons tomato purée

Peel, pip and chop the tomatoes and stir them, with the tomato purée into the sauce.

½ glass stock or water

Moisten with warm liquid, cover and cook over low heat for 2 hours, adding liquid if necessary. (The sauce should be rather thick.)

juice of ½ lemon

Remove the pork rind, bay leaf and any unwanted fat. Strain the sauce and sharpen it with lemon juice.

Veal and Ham au Gratin Expensive

1½ lb fillet of veal ✦ 1

Heat the fat in a flameproof casserole

tablespoon fat ✦ 1 carrot 1 onion ✦ a stick of celery a bouquet garni ✦ ½ glass white wine	and lightly brown the meat, and the vegetables cut in small pieces. Sprinkle with white wine, cover and cook gently for 30 to 40 minutes. (The meat should be rosy, not overcooked.)
2 tablespoons butter ✦ 2 tablespoons flour ✦ 1½ glasses milk ✦ salt and pepper ✦ 5 oz grated cheese	Meanwhile, work the butter and flour together in a small saucepan over low heat. Stir in the milk little by little, being careful to avoid lumps. Cook slowly for 15 minutes, add the cheese, warm through, season and lift the pan from the fire.
4 slices ham ✦ 8 thin slices gruyère cheese	Slice the veal thinly. Cut the pieces of ham in two. In a fireproof dish arrange alternate slices of veal, ham and cheese, overlapping, and cover them with sauce.
2 tablespoons grated cheese ✦ 2 tablespoons melted butter	Sprinkle with cheese and melted butter and brown in a hot oven (425° F, 220° C, Gas 7) for ½ hour.

Stuffed Breast of Veal Economical

Have the breast boned by the butcher and keep the bones for stock.

This dish, which will serve 6 people, is made by slitting the breast down its length and filling it with stuffing. Veal has a tendency to dry up in the oven, so we suggest that you braise both this dish and the cheaper version mentioned below.

2 slices bread ✦ 2 tablespoons white wine ✦ 1 calf's kidney	Soak, squeeze and crumble the bread into a bowl. Cut the kidney in two, remove the white core, dip it in boiling water, wipe it dry and chop it.
4 oz kidney fat ✦ 1 egg salt and pepper ✦ 1 tablespoon minced parsley 2 lb breast of veal ✦ a bard of back pork fat	Chop the kidney fat and mix it with the bread, kidney, egg and seasoning. Stuff the breast and sew it up. Wrap the meat in the bard and secure it with string.
2 carrots ✦ 1 onion ✦ a stalk of celery ✦ 1 tablespoon fat	Put the vegetables, chopped, into a flameproof casserole with the fat and place the meat on top. Cover and cook gently for 10 minutes.

½ glass white wine	Pour the white wine down the side of the casserole and let it reduce to half with the lid off.
1 glass veal stock ✦ a bouquet garni	Add the warm stock and the bouquet, cover and simmer for 2 hours. Remove the bard and the string. Slice the meat and serve it on a hot dish covered with its own sauce, strained and cleared of surplus fat.

Serve with potato purée and spinach, or sorrel.

Breast of veal can be cooked in the same way with a more economical stuffing made of sausage meat mixed with bread (previously soaked in a little stock) an egg, minced onion or shallots softened in butter, and chopped parsley.

Veal with Tunny Expensive

This is an Italian dish, excellent in summer and very useful for a cold buffet. The anchovies give the veal a special flavour, but they are not essential.

Prepare this dish a day or two in advance.

2 salted anchovies	Wash the anchovies well. Remove heads, tails and bones, and chop them up.
1¾ lb fillet of veal	Insert the anchovies into slits in the meat.
a bay leaf ✦ 1 onion ✦ 2 cloves ✦ 2 carrots ✦ 1½ pints water ✦ 1 glass white wine ✦ salt and pepper	Stick the cloves through the bay leaf and into the onion. Put the vegetables, water, wine and seasoning into a flame-proof casserole and bring to the boil. Put the meat into the boiling liquid (which must cover it). Reduce the heat and simmer for 1½ hours with the lid on. Lift out the meat, drain and wipe it dry, and put it in a deep dish.
a 4 oz tin tunny ✦ 2 or 3 anchovy fillets ✦ 1 glass olive oil ✦ the juice of ½ lemon ✦ 1 or 2 teaspoons capers, coarsely chopped ✦ pepper	Pound or blend the tunny with the anchovies. Stir in the oil little by little to make a thick sauce. Add the lemon juice and capers, stirring all the time. The sauce must be creamy and fairly liquid. Season, and pour it over the

meat. Marinade in a cool place from 24 to 48 hours.

Before serving, cut the veal in fairly thin slices and cover them with sauce.

You can also slice the meat as soon as it is cooked. In this case, let it cool and then marinade it for only 24 hours.

Chops and Escalopes

Chops. If they are to be tender and juicy, veal chops should not be cut too thin. You can even buy an extra thick chop—rather like a Châteaubriand steak—and divide it between two people.

Veal is cut up in very much the same way as mutton and lamb. There are two kinds of chops from the loin—chump, which has hardly any bone, and loin chop with a compact little 'nut' of meat. The price is about the same. Cutlets come from the best end of neck.

Preparation. Veal chops are best sautéd in butter and served with their own juice. They can also be grilled, but in this case they must be brushed with plenty of melted butter and basted abundantly. Remember, grill gently and baste often.

How to serve veal cutlets. The cutlet bones look nicer if they are trimmed with paper frills which are sold ready-made, or can easily be made at home, like this:

Take some fairly thin white paper
Cut it in pieces measuring about 5×8 inches
Pile them one on top of another
Fold them in half lengthwise
With scissors, or a sharp knife, make cuts about $\frac{3}{4}$-inch deep at $\frac{1}{4}$-inch intervals along the folded edge
Separate the two edges of paper and fold them the other way round, so that the slit parts bow out
Roll a frill round each bone and tie it in place with thread.

Veal Chops à la Bourguignonne Expensive

4 veal chops ✦ flour 1 tablespoon fat	Season the chops. Flour them generously and brown them on both sides in a flameproof casserole.
8 button mushrooms ✦ 6 small onions ✦ 4 oz diced bacon ✦ 1 clove garlic, crushed	Arrange the mushrooms, onion, garlic and bacon round the meat and brown them lightly.
½ glass red wine ✦ ¼ glass bouillon	Trickle in the wine and let it reduce to half. Add the warm bouillon, cover, and cook gently for 10 minutes.
½ teaspoon chopped parsley	Sprinkle with parsley and serve.

Veal Chops with Paprika Expensive

4 veal chops ✦ salt 1 tablespoon flour	Salt the chops and coat them with flour.
1 tablespoon lard 5 onions	Heat the lard in a flameproof casserole. Brown the chops and lift them out. Slice the onions, let them soften in the casserole, with the lid on, for 10 minutes. Replace the meat.
2 tablespoons paprika ✦ a pinch cayenne pepper (optional) ✦ ½ glass bouillon	Sprinkle it with paprika and pepper. Moisten with bouillon. Cover and cook on a very low fire for ¾ hour.
3 tablespoons fresh cream lemon juice	Remove any unwanted fat from the sauce. Add the cream and lemon, taking care that the sauce does not boil.

Veal Cutlets (or Escalopes) en Papillottes Expensive

Take some foil or greaseproof paper and cut out 4 large hearts, each when folded in two being about ¾-inch larger all round than the cutlet or escalope.

Lay them side by side on the table with the points towards you. Oil the greaseproof paper lightly. (This is not necessary with foil.)

If you choose escalopes, they should be small and fairly thick.

2 tablespoons fat ✦ 4 escalopes (or cutlets)	Heat the fat in a frying pan and brown the meat on both sides. Lift it out.

a little butter ✦ 4 shallots 8 small mushrooms ✦ 2 tablespoons white wine salt and pepper ✦ 1 teaspoon minced parsley	Add a little butter to the pan and brown the shallots and mushrooms, which you have chopped very finely. Moisten with white wine, season, and simmer for a few minutes. Sprinkle with parsley.
4 slices ham	Cut each slice of ham in two. Sandwich the veal between two layers of vegetables and two half slices of ham. Lay each sandwich on one side of a foil or paper heart (the cutlet bone should point towards you) fold, and roll over the edges securely. Arrange the papillottes on a fireproof dish. Put them in a moderate oven (355° F, 180° C, Gas 4) for 10 minutes if they are wrapped in paper or 20 minutes if in foil. Remove the coverings and serve.

Veal Chops with Mushrooms and Cream Expensive

4 veal chops ✦ 1 tablespoon flour ✦ salt and pepper ✦ 2 tablespoons butter	Season and flour the chops. Brown them in hot butter, in a frying pan.
12 small mushrooms ✦ salt and pepper ✦ 1 teaspoon flour ✦ ½ glass white wine	Surround the meat with finely-sliced and well-seasoned mushrooms. As soon as these are browned, dust with flour and add the wine. Stir, cover and simmer for 10 minutes.
2 tablespoons sherry (or madeira) ✦ 4 tablespoons fresh cream ✦ ½ teaspoon minced parsley	Put the veal on a hot dish. Pour the sherry and cream over the mushrooms and heat, without letting the sauce boil. Cover the meat with mushroom sauce and dust with parsley.

Escalopes. An escalope is a slice cut from a lean piece of veal. It is difficult to persuade a butcher to cut an escalope correctly, on the bias, from an expensive cut as he is left with awkward pieces which he must sell at a loss.

If you can buy the whole of the leg muscle which corresponds to the roll of the silverside in beef, and cut your own escalopes, you can use the diminishing ends of your piece of meat for grenadins (smaller but thicker than escalopes) and médaillons, which are miniature escalopes. However you buy them, escalopes are expensive, but in this way they will at least be good.

Escalopes with Mushrooms à l'Italienne Expensive

1 teaspoon oil ✦ 1 teaspoon butter ✦ 1 clove garlic ✦ a bay leaf	Heat the oil and butter in a frying pan with the garlic and bay leaf.
4 escalopes veal ✦ salt and pepper	Cut the escalopes in pieces about 1½-inch square. Season, and sauté them rapidly.
8 or 10 mushrooms ✦ 1 teaspoon butter	Add the finely-sliced mushrooms and butter to the meat, and continue cooking. Remove the garlic and bay leaf. Place the meat on a hot dish, covered with mushrooms.
the juice of ½ lemon ✦ 1 tablespoon bouillon or water	Deglaze the pan with lemon juice and bouillon, scraping it well with a wooden spoon. Stir and cook for a moment or two. Pour the sauce over the meat, and serve.

Like the Saltimboca on p. 93 this dish can be made with the small, untidy pieces left when you have cut escalopes diagonally from a piece of meat.

Escalopes à la Viennoise (Wiener Schnitzel) Expensive

Escalopes à la Viennoise must be light and crisp. The slices should be cut on the bias, an even ¼-inch thick, and carefully flattened to half that thickness.

4 escalopes ✦ juice of 1 lemon	Marinate the escalopes in lemon juice for 1 hour, turning them occasionally.
1 egg ✦ salt and pepper 1 teaspoon oil ✦ 1 teaspoon water	Beat all together lightly in a soup plate.
breadcrumbs	Put the breadcrumbs in another soup plate. Dry the escalopes, dip them in the egg mixture and then in breadcrumbs, pressing them on firmly.

4 oz butter ✦ 6 fillets anchovy ✦ a pinch paprika (optional)

Crush the anchovies with a fork. Melt the butter in a frying pan and stir in the anchovies and paprika. Cook gently 4 or 5 minutes. Raise the heat, taking care that the butter does not burn, and fry the escalopes rapidly.

Serve with quarters of lemon and fried parsley (p. 68).

Saltimboca Expensive

4 very thin escalopes ✦ 4 slices ham (raw if possible) 2 leaves sage ✦ salt and pepper

Cut the escalopes and the slices of ham in pieces about 2-inches square. Chop the sage and sprinkle it, together with seasoning, on one side of the meat. Cover each piece of veal with a slice of ham and secure with a toothpick.

2 tablespoons butter

Melt the butter in a frying pan and cook the saltimboca 2 minutes on the ham side and 4 minutes on the veal. Put them, ham-side-up on a heated dish.

1 tablespoon butter ✦ 1 tablespoon sherry or white wine

Stir the wine and butter into the caramel in the pan, heat and pour over the meat.

Stuffed Escalopes Moderately expensive

2 escalopes, halved ✦ 4 slices bread ✦ 2 tablespoons butter (or more)

Trim the bread to the same size as the escalopes and fry. Adding more butter if necessary, fry the veal, and put each halved escalope on a piece of fried bread.

4 mushrooms ✦ 1 clove garlic ✦ 1 slice chopped ham ✦ 6 oz cold meat or chicken (not mutton)

Brown the chopped mushrooms in the pan, add the garlic, ham, and chopped cold meat, mix together and brown.

1 tablespoon tomato purée salt and pepper ✦ 2 tablespoons fresh cream ✦ 1 tablespoon breadcrumbs

Stir in the tomato purée and let it bubble. Add the cream, but see that the sauce does not boil. Spread the mixture over each halved escalope. Top with breadcrumbs.

2 tablespoons melted butter
½ glass white wine

Sprinkle with melted butter and brown in the oven, or under the grill.
Meanwhile, deglaze the pan with wine. Simmer a moment or two, and serve the sauce with the meat.

Ragoûts of Veal

Shoulder of veal, breast, knuckle, middle neck and trimmings from other cuts can be made into various delicious stews and casseroles which we have grouped under the name of ragoûts.

These are divided into two main groups: blanquettes, which are light in colour, and ragoûts, which are coloured by browning the meat in hot fat and sprinkling it with flour which in turn is allowed to brown before adding hot liquid. Never let a ragoût boil, just simmer gently.

Buying veal for ragoûts. Ready-cut 'pie veal' is on sale, but it is better to choose your own piece of meat and have it cut—or cut it yourself. The table on p. 78 will show you which pieces of veal are suitable. Choosing your own meat will probably be a little more expensive, but you will know what you are buying and much less of the surface will have been exposed to the air.

You will need for each person 6–8 oz of boned meat or about 12 oz with bone.

Simple Blanquettes de Veau Economical

1¾ lb veal cut in large pieces ✦ salt

Put the meat in a large saucepan. Cover it with cold water, bring to the boil with the lid on, skim and salt.

6 small onions ✦ 2 quartered carrots ✦ 1 clove garlic ✦ a bouquet garni

Simmer the vegetables with the meat for 1½ hours.

2 tablespoons butter
3 tablespoons flour

15 minutes before the veal is done, work the butter and flour together over a low heat and stir in, little by little, 2 glasses of the liquid from the meat. Cook very gently for 15 minutes.

2 yolks of egg ✦ 2 tablespoons fresh cream

Whisk the eggs and cream together in a bowl, adding gradually a little hot sauce. When the egg yolks have thickened mix them with the rest of the sauce. Continue to whip over the fire for 2 minutes. Season.

juice of ½ lemon ✦ salt and pepper ✦ ½ teaspoon chopped parsley

Drain the meat and remove any pieces of fat and bone. Put it into a hot dish and cover with sauce. Sprinkle with parsley and serve.

Saute de Veau Printaniére Expensive

This is a dish to make with the new vegetables in spring.

3 tablespoons fat ✦ 1¾ lb veal ✦ 2 tablespoons flour

Melt the fat in a flameproof casserole. Cut the meat in large squares and brown it all over. Dredge with flour and let this colour.

1 glass white wine* ✦ 1 glass stock or water ✦ salt and pepper ✦ a bouquet garni

Pour the wine down the side of the casserole. Let it reduce for 5 minutes. Add the stock and seasoning. Cover and simmer for 1 hour.

8 carrots ✦ 8 young turnips ✦ 10 small onions ✦ 1 cup fresh peas ✦ 12 new potatoes ✦ salt and pepper

Add the vegetables and cook for another ½ hour.

1 tablespoon chopped chives, parsley and chervil

Sprinkle with herbs and serve.

* If you prefer to omit the wine, use 1½ glasses of stock and do not let it reduce.

Matelote de Veau Economical

1¾ lb stewing veal ✦ 3 tablespoons flour ✦ 2 tablespoons fat ✦ 1 onion

Cut the veal into 2-inch squares and dip it in flour. Heat the fat in a flameproof casserole and brown the meat. Add the sliced onion. Dust with the rest of the flour, and let it colour.

2 cloves garlic, crushed salt and pepper ✦ a bouquet garni ✦ 1 glass red wine

Add herbs and seasoning, pour in the wine, and let it reduce to half, with the lid off.

1½ glasses veal stock

Warm the veal stock and pour it into the casserole. Cover and simmer for 1½ hours.

5 or 6 small onions ✦ 12 button mushrooms ✦ 1 tablespoon butter

Brown the onions and mushrooms in butter and cook them for a further ½ hour together with the meat.

1 teaspoon chopped parsley

Serve, sprinkled with parsley.

Veal and Noodles au Gratin Economical

This dish can be prepared in advance and put in the oven half an hour before the meal.

2 tablespoons flour ✦ salt and pepper ✦ 1¾ lb veal cut in small cubes ✦ 2 tablespoons fat

Mix flour and seasoning in a soup plate and toss with the meat. Brown the meat all over in a large saucepan.

1 onion ✦ 2 tomatoes ✦ 1 glass stock

Chop finely the onion and the tomatoes, less skin and pips. Add them to the meat. Moisten with stock, cover and simmer for ¾ hour.

½ lb noodles

Meanwhile cook the noodles for 10 minutes in boiling, salted water. Drain and put them, mixed with the meat, in a buttered fireproof dish.

5 oz fresh cream (or a cup of cheese sauce)

Pour over the cream or sauce and sprinkle with grated cheese and breadcrumbs. Cook, covered with a lid or a piece of foil, for 20 minutes in a moderate oven (355° F, 180° C, Gas 5). Uncover and brown for 10 minutes.

Djuvee Economical

This is a Yugoslav dish. Use neck, shoulder or breast of veal, and shoulder or belly of pork with as much fat as possible removed.

2 onions ✦ 2 green peppers
1 tablespoon oil

Remove the seeds from the peppers and chop them with the onions. Brown together in a frying pan. Arrange them in the bottom of a deep, fireproof dish.

4 tomatoes ✦ salt and pepper

Chop the tomatoes after you have removed the skin and pips. Season, and put half into the fireproof dish.

1 cup uncooked rice

Adding, if necessary, a little oil to the frying pan, cook the rice, shaking all

	the time, until it is golden brown. Put it into the dish with the rest of the tomatoes on top.
¾ lb veal ✦ ¾ lb pork ✦ salt and pepper	Cut the meat into 1-inch cubes. Brown them in the frying pan. Season, and arrange them in the dish.
2 glasses veal stock	Pour the warmed stock over the meat. Cover with foil or a lid and cook in a moderate oven (355° F, 180° C, Gas 4) for 1½ hours.
½ teaspoon paprika (optional)	Sprinkle with paprika before serving.

Veal with Oranges Moderately expensive

This is a Swedish dish.

1¾ lb veal ✦ 2 tablespoons butter	Cut the veal in long, thin strips. Heat the butter in a frying pan and cook the meal for 3 minutes on each side. Put it into a buttered casserole.
2 tablespoons grated parmesan ✦ salt and pepper ½ teaspoon caster sugar	Mix all together and sprinkle over the meat, using plenty of pepper.
2 carrots ✦ 2 oranges	Slice the carrots. Peel the oranges and cut them in fine slices. Arrange them on top of the meat.
1 glass stock	Add the stock. Cover the casserole and cook in a slow oven (335° F, 170° C, Gas 3) for 1¼ hours.
3 tablespoons sherry	Sprinkle with sherry and continue to cook for 15 minutes with the lid off.

Crisped Breast of Veal Economical

1¾ lb breast of veal ✦ salt	Put the veal into cold, salted water and bring it to the boil in a large saucepan.
1 carrot ✦ 1 onion ✦ 2 stalks celery ✦ 1 bouquet garni	As soon as the water boils add the vegetables, coarsely chopped, and the bouquet garni. Cook for 1¼ hours with the lid not quite closed. Lift out the meat.
a pinch nutmeg ✦ salt ✦ 1 teaspoon minced parsley	Cut the meat in 1½-inch cubes. Let it marinate with the other ingredients for

3 tablespoons olive oil juice of ½ lemon ✦ 5 crushed peppercorns

3 hours, turning from time to time. Drain and dry the meat.

1 tablespoon flour ✦ 1 teaspoon oil ✦ 1 teaspoon water ✦ 1 egg ✦ breadcrumbs

Dip the meat first in flour, then egg beaten with oil and water. Finally, roll the meat cubes in breadcrumbs and put them in a buttered fireproof dish. Season.

Cook in a moderate oven (380° F, 195 C, Gas 5) turning once, until the pieces of meat are browned all over. Serve with a spicy sauce.

Paupiettes of Veal

Paupiettes of veal are prepared in the same way as those of beef (p. 75). It is better to allow two small paupiettes for each person rather than one large.

Paupiettes of Veal with Anchovies Moderately expensive

8 thin slices veal ✦ 8 small slices gruyère cheese ✦ 8 anchovy fillets ✦ pepper

Put a slice of cheese, an anchovy fillet and a sprinkling of pepper on each slice of veal. Roll and tie them.

3 tablespoons butter

Heat the butter in a frying pan and brown the paupiettes. Cover and cook for 20 minutes. Put them on a dish and keep them hot.

1 tablespoon white wine 1 tablespoon water ✦ 1 teaspoon butter ✦ salt if necessary

Stir the wine and water into the caramel in the frying pan, scraping it well with a wooden spoon. Correct the seasoning. Add the butter, stir again and pour the sauce over the meat.

NOTE: Where bacon or anchovies are used in a dish one must always use salt with caution. Some butter is so salty that it also calls for special care.

Paupiettes en Brochettes Moderately expensive

8 thin slices veal ✦ juice of ½ lemon ✦ salt and pepper

Season the meat and sprinkle it with lemon juice, salt and pepper.

2 thick slices of ham
8 thin rashers bacon

Cut each slice of ham in four and roll a piece inside each paupiette. Wrap each one in a rasher of bacon.

4 slices bread ✦ 2 tablespoons melted butter	Remove the crusts, and cut each slice of bread in two, sprinkling with melted butter.
8 sage leaves	Thread the paupiettes, alternately with a slice of bread and a sage leaf, on to four skewers. Sprinkle them with melted butter, and bake them in a moderate oven (355° F, 180° C, Gas 4) for ½ hour, turning the skewers halfway through.

Paupiettes with Paprika Moderately expensive

Use Hungarian bacon for this recipe if you can get it. Otherwise ordinary bacon will do.

a rather thick slice of bacon 1 teaspoon paprika	Cut the bacon into 8 strips and roll them in paprika, pressing it well in.
8 thin slices of veal ✦ salt	Salt each slice of veal lightly and roll it round a strip of bacon, securing it with string.
4 onions ✦ 1 tablespoon lard ✦ 3 teaspoons paprika a pinch cayenne pepper	Chop the onions finely and brown them with the paupiettes in a flameproof casserole. Adjust the seasoning and sprinkle with paprika and cayenne pepper.
½ glass stock ✦ 3 tablespoons sour cream	Stir in the stock. Cover and cook on a slow fire for ¾ hour. Add the cream just before serving, being careful that the sauce does not boil.

Paupiettes of Veal with Chicken Livers Expensive

1 tablespoon butter 4 chicken livers	Heat the butter in a frying pan and sauter the chicken livers gently.
2 slices of ham (raw if possible) ✦ 1 sage leaf ½ teaspoon each of chopped parsley and chives ✦ salt and pepper	Chop the ham, chicken livers and sage and mix with the herbs. Season.
8 thin slices veal ✦ 1 tablespoon flour	Spread each slice of veal with the savoury mixture. Roll, tie and coat with flour.

1 tablespoon butter
½ glass sherry or white wine

Brown the paupiettes in butter. Pour in the wine, stirring well, and let it bubble until the sauce is like a thick syrup.

8 slices bread ✦ 2 tablespoons butter ✦ 2 tablespoons stock or water

Fry the bread in butter and put the slices on a hot dish. Put a paupiette on each. Deglaze the pan, and when the sauce has boiled for a moment or two pour it over the paupiettes and serve.

Paupiettes with Cheese and Ham Expensive

8 thin slices veal ✦ 4 large slices ham (raw if possible) ✦ 4 oz gruyère cheese

Cut the veal in 1½- to 2-inch squares, and the ham in pieces of the same size. Divide the gruyère into 8 pieces.

salt and pepper

Season the meat and top each piece with ham and cheese. Roll and tie.

2 tablespoons butter

Fry the paupiettes in butter for 10 minutes turning all the time. Cover and cook gently for 10 minutes more. Put them on a dish to keep hot.

1 teaspoon butter ✦ ½ teaspoon cornflour ✦ ½ glass sherry, marsala, madeira or dry white wine

Melt the butter in the pan you have been using and sift in the cornflour. Add the wine, scraping the bottom of the pan as you do so. Cook 3 minutes over low heat and pour the sauce over the paupiettes.

Paupiettes with Salt Pork Moderately expensive

1 onion ✦ 1 clove garlic
1 teaspoon fat

Chop the onion and garlic finely and let them soften in the hot fat without colouring.

a scant 6 oz salt pork ✦ salt (with caution) and pepper

Soak the salt pork in cold water for ½ hour then drain and chop it. Mix it with the onion and garlic, and season.

4 slices veal ✦ 2 tablespoons fat ✦ 1 onion ✦ 1 carrot ✦ a branch celery

Roll and tie the veal round the stuffing to make paupiettes. Brown them all over in fat. Surround with coarsely chopped vegetables and let them brown.

½ glass white wine

Pour the wine over the paupiettes and reduce it a little over gentle heat.

1 tablespoon tomato purée ½ glass stock ✦ salt and pepper	Dilute the tomato purée with stock, add it to the liquid in the pan. Season, cover, and cook on a low fire for ½ hour, basting the paupiettes from time to time.
2 tomatoes ✦ 1 tablespoon oil	Cut the tomatoes in two and brown them in oil. Put the paupiettes on a dish with a half tomato on each. Strain the sauce over them.

This dish looks attractive if the paupiettes are arranged, alternately with heaps of French beans, round a mound of small, boiled potatoes sprinkled with chopped parsley.

You can use sausage meat instead of salt pork if you wish.

USUAL CUTS OF LAMB AND MUTTON IN LONDON AND THE HOME COUNTIES

(Price comparisons apply to both lamb and mutton.
Lamb is the dearer of the two, and home-killed more expensive than New Zealand)

Cut	Position	Characteristics	Cooking Suggestions
Leg	Hind leg of the animal.	The dearest roasting cut. It is leaner and drier than shoulder but there is less waste. Often divided into fillet and knuckle (or shank) end, the latter having more bone but a sweeter flavour. Leg of lamb weighs 4–5½ lb.	Roast or boiled. May be boned and stuffed. Slices cut across the fillet end of leg can be fried or grilled, or cubed to make kebabs.
Loin (whole)	Middle of back, corresponding to sirloin.	Rather cheaper than leg. Saddle of lamb, which weighs approximately 6 lb, is a favourite banquet dish. Usually divided down the back into two separate joints, or into chops. If boned and rolled, weighs 3–4 lb.	May be roasted on the bone, or boned, stuffed and rolled. Can be cut and tied into noisettes.
Chump Chops	From leg end of loin.	Slightly more expensive per lb than loin.	Usually grilled or fried.

Cut	Position	Characteristics	Cooking Suggestions
Loin Chops	From rib end of loin.	Sold with or without kidney. Tenderer than chump chops, but more bone is wasted.	Usually grilled or fried.
Best End of Neck	Ribs adjoining the loin.	Sold whole at a medium price, or divided into cutlets which are sometimes little cheaper than chops. Lamb meat is very sweet. Weight, 1–2 lb.	May be roasted or braised. Cutlets are usually grilled or sautéd.
Middle neck	Fore end of ribs and base of neck.	Cheaper cut. Occasionally two or three chops are cut from rib end. Choose a joint with medium amount of fat and not too much gristle.	Suitable for stewing, casseroles and soups.
Neck (scrag)	Neck adjoining head.	Cheapest portion of the animal (except for breast). Rather coarse and fairly wasteful. Usually sold with middle neck.	As above.

LAMB AND MUTTON (continued)

Cut	Position	Characteristics	Cooking Suggestions
Shoulder	Front leg and shoulder.	Usually the cheapest of the roasting joints. Slightly fat but very sweet in flavour. Difficult to carve unless boned.	May be roasted whole, or boned and stuffed, or braised. Cut into cubes, it can be used for curries, blanquettes or stews.
Blade half shoulder Knuckle end of shoulder		Shoulder may be divided into blade half and knuckle end, the former being slightly the more expensive.	As above.
Breast	Underneath the animal between the four legs.	Extremely cheap, but rather fat. May be boned, stuffed and rolled.	Filled with a home-made herb stuffing (especially if no extra fat is added) it makes a pleasant joint for roasting or braising. As a stew it is rather fat.

LAMB AND MUTTON

THE tables on pages 102, 103 and 104 show the positions of the various cuts and their characteristics, together with some suggestions for cooking.

LAMB AND MUTTON

Lamb is meat from an animal of either sex not more than twelve months old. Most New Zealand lambs are slaughtered for export at four to six months, but many home-grown lambs are killed much later and may weigh as much as 50–60 lb. All lamb from New Zealand is now clearly stamped 'NEW ZEALAND LAMB', and mutton is marked merely 'NEW ZEALAND'. By this admirable arrangement you know just what you are buying.

Lamb is tenderer than mutton and far less fat, and its colour, whether frozen or fresh is more attractive. The size of the joints is also more suitable for present-day housekeeping.

In many shops mutton is so scarce that one is tempted to believe that very few sheep grow up. In fact, large quantities of mutton are bought on contract by the Services, schools, institutions, etc., but many retail butchers are shy of selling it since, for the reasons we have mentioned, lamb is so much more popular with their customers. Moreover, mutton is tough unless it is hung, and while hanging it changes colour and begins to look unattractive. During the war, owing to the extreme difficulty of obtaining meat, people were obliged to buy mutton which had not been hung and butchers still have bitter memories of the complaints about toughness which resulted. This is a pity, since mutton used to be one of the glories of traditional English cooking.

The best of our home-grown mutton comes from Southdown sheep or from the Scottish and Welsh mountain breeds whose meat has a richer and more gamey flavour. Flavour depends, to a large extent, on the pasture on which animals have fed. An example of this is the famous *pré-salé* mutton from sheep which have grazed on the salt marshes along the French coast.

Mutton, especially the neck and loin, has a great deal of fat distributed through the meat. This makes it rather wasteful, though a proportion of fat will ensure that the meat is succulent and well-flavoured. The taste of mutton dripping is too strong for most purposes and, apart from smearing it on skiing boots (it keeps the leather waterproof without softening it too much), we have not found a really satisfactory use for it.

All mutton and lamb, like other meat, should be gently and thoroughly thawed out at room temperature before cooking.

How to choose your meat. The best mutton is plump and small-boned with a loin wide in proportion, and legs thick and stocky rather than rangy and long. The lean is not such a strong red as beef and has a slightly brownish tinge. It should be well hung, and after hanging the cut surface sometimes takes a purplish tinge. Mutton flesh should be firm and close-textured and the fat hard, white and waxy. Poor quality mutton has coarse, yellow fat and the lean is greyish.

Good quality lamb should have bright red flesh and a fair proportion of white fat. A great deal of imported meat, both separate cuts and whole sides, is now being packed in a plastic wrapping which prevents it from drying unduly during transit.

Lamb bones, which are lighter and more brittle than those of mutton, should be slightly translucent, and the kidney firm, without any unpleasant smell.

The French are fond of sucking lambs which are killed at about 5–6 weeks old and weigh in the region of 6–8 lb. Certain

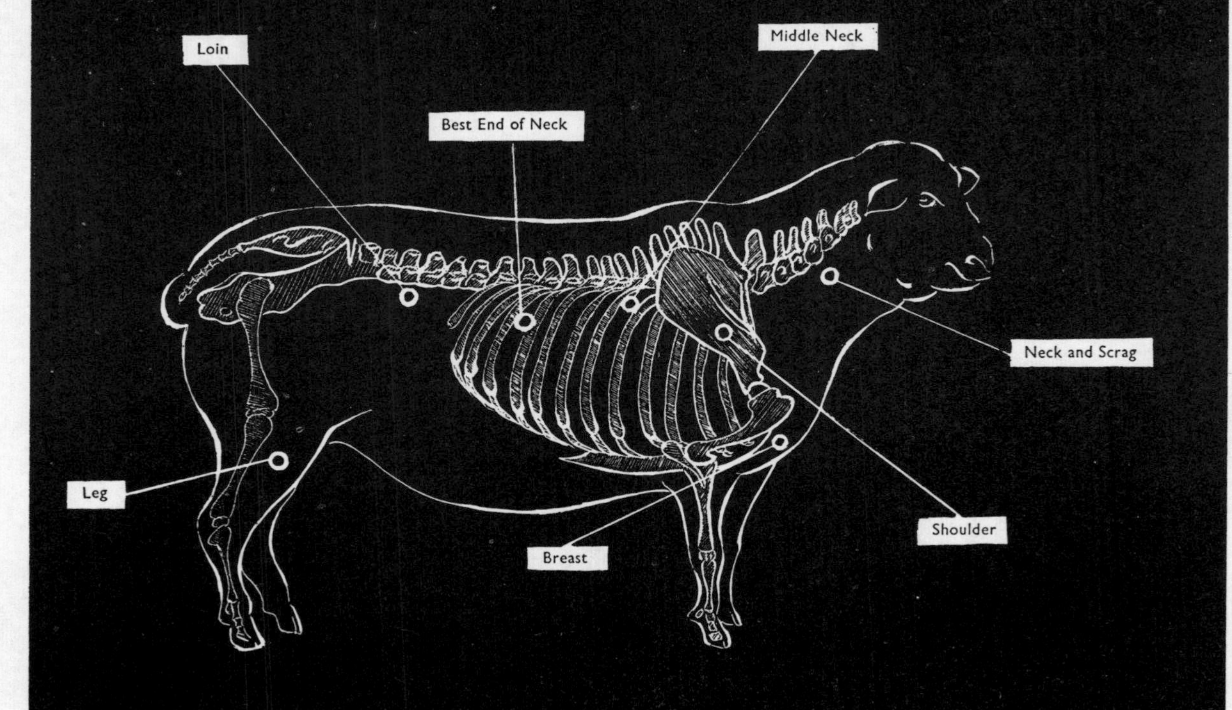
Loin
Middle Neck
Best End of Neck
Neck and Scrag
Leg
Shoulder
Breast

English butchers will order these '*Pauillac*' lambs for their customers during early spring.

Roasting lamb and mutton. Mutton and lamb are excellent roasted or grilled and need very little extra fat. They can be roasted in a moderate oven at 380° F (195° C, Gas 4) for 30 minutes to the lb, or slow roasted at 335° F (170° C, Gas 3) for 40 minutes per lb.

The New Zealand Information Bureau in their leaflet recommend putting lamb into a cold oven set at 350° F (180° C, Gas 4) and cooking it for 30–35 minutes to the lb. If the joint is stuffed, they allow 40–45 minutes to each lb.

Roast mutton is usually served well done and lamb, though care must be taken not to overcook it, should not be underdone.

A little seasoned flour rubbed into the surface of the joint will absorb the surplus fat and give a beautiful golden-brown finish.

Accompaniments. Lamb goes best with new potatoes, spring vegetables, green peas, button onions, French beans, mint sauce and clear gravy.

Mutton is good with roast potatoes, young turnips or haricot beans, rowan, cranberry or red currant jelly, and caper or onion sauce. The French sometimes serve mutton with horseradish sauce.

How to serve mutton and lamb. It is important to see that surplus fat is trimmed away before mutton is brought to table in order to avoid a depressing fringe of discarded fat round the plates. Mutton fat congeals quickly and becomes unattractive, so gravy must be carefully skimmed and plates and dishes well heated. The most fastidious Victorians brought gravy spoons to table in silver nautilus shells filled with boiling water—an idea as practical as it is decorative.

Leg of Lamb or Mutton

Leg of lamb or mutton is the dearest roasting cut from the animal. In these days of smaller families legs are often sold halved, the knuckle having a sweeter flavour but more bone than the fillet end. Slices of fillet cut from the leg can be grilled or fried.

To cook a leg. Roasting is the most usual way. If you are fond of garlic don't forget to tuck a clove into the fat near the knuckle.

A leg may also be boiled, usually for 25 minutes to the lb and 25 minutes over, or poached very gently for hours and hours until it is tender enough to cut with a spoon.

The French sometimes marinade a leg of mutton for a day or two (p. 111). The joint is excellent roasted on a bed of potatoes and onions, finely sliced, and served with French beans, or noodles mixed with the juice which has run out of the meat.

How to carve a leg of lamb or mutton. Lamb and mutton should not be carved in such thin slices as beef. With the carving fork firmly fixed in the knuckle flesh, which is to your left, make a vertical cut right down to the bone. Carve slices between ¼- and ½-inch thick and slightly wedge-shaped. Some people like a little knuckle with their helping of meat from the centre.

The French sometimes carve a leg of lamb in long slices parallel to the bone, keeping them rather thin. These long slices are not so juicy as the shorter, thicker ones.

Shoulder of Lamb or Mutton

Shoulder is a cheaper joint than leg, but it is very fat and rather awkward to carve unless it is boned. The meat has a very delicate flavour.

How to buy a shoulder. Choose a joint with a small knucklebone. The butcher will, if you wish, remove the bone and some butchers sell shoulders already rolled and stuffed. Such joints should only be bought from a butcher in whom you have confidence. You will then feel sure that the stuffing is of good quality and that no inferior meat has been included with your joint. You can, if you wish, buy half a shoulder.

In France, shoulder of mutton is often seasoned, stuffed, and sold rolled or '*en ballot*', tied with string into an elegant globe.

Owing to the high proportion of bone you should allow about 1 lb of unboned shoulder for each person.

How to prepare a shoulder. This joint is usually roasted, either on the bone or boned, stuffed and rolled. Occasionally it is braised. If you wish to stuff it, allow a good 4 oz of stuffing to each pound of meat.

Shoulder can, of course, be treated in other ways but, although the flavour is very sweet, the high proportion of fat makes this cut a little wasteful.

Carving. The meat should be placed on a dish so that the fleshiest part is upwards. Keeping the projecting shank bone to your left, start carving in the centre and work outwards, gradually turning the knife so as to take small slices from each side of the bladebone, and small slices parallel to the shank bone. When there is no more meat on top, turn the joint over and cut horizontal slices.

Saddle, Loin and Best End of Neck

Saddle and loin are rather expensive but very good. Roast saddle of mutton used to be a favourite dish at banquets and saddle of lamb was popular with Victorian families, but few people nowadays want such a large joint. The saddle consists of both sides of the loin joined by the backbone.

Buying saddle, loin and best end of neck. Saddle of lamb usually weighs 4½–8 lb, and saddle of mutton about 8–11 lb. The loin weighs about half.

Best end of neck should be chined by the butcher. This means sawing through the chine bone, or split backbone, so that it can be removed immediately before carving. Like this you can divide the joint into chops or carve it into thin slices.

If you should have to cater for a large number of people, a whole hindquarter of lamb (leg and loin) or forequarter (shoulder, scrag and best end of neck, with or without breast) is an excellent buy. The hindquarter is the more economical, while the forequarter is considered the more delicate.

Allow about ¾–1 lb of meat with bone for each person.

Preparation. Saddle is a roasting joint. Loin of mutton, marinaded with a piquant sauce, makes an excellent barbecue, whilst loin of lamb is better simply roasted, or divided into chops and fried or grilled.

Carving. Saddle is carved with the grain of the meat. Holding the joint firmly with a carving fork, make two long cuts each side of and parallel to the backbone and continue cutting wedge-shaped slices which can be divided in half if they are too long.

Loin and best end of neck are carved parallel with the rib bones.

Mutton Marinaded and Roast Moderately expensive

about 2 lb leg or shoulder with bone ✦ 4 cloves garlic ✦ 2 tablespoons oil

Insert pieces of garlic into the meat, here and there. Sprinkle with oil.

1 onion ✦ 1 carrot ✦ 4 cloves ✦ 4 stalks celery ✦ salt and 6 peppercorns ✦ ½ glass vinegar ✦ 1½ glasses white wine (optional)

Put the meat and the sliced vegetables into a deep dish with the wine and vinegar and marinade for 24 hours, turning from time to time. Drain the mutton and wipe it dry.

1 tablespoon oil ✦ 1 tablespoon caster sugar *or* 1 teaspoon honey

Set the meat on a roasting tin and brush it with oil. Put it in a hot oven for 15 minutes (425° F, 220° C, Gas 7) then brush it with caster sugar or honey. Meanwhile, boil the marinade until it is reduced to half, and strain. Pour it over the mutton and, once this is brown, continue roasting at a lower temperature (355° F, 180° C, Gas 4). If you prefer mutton not too well done, 15 minutes to the lb should be sufficient.

Crown Roast Moderately expensive

This crown roast should serve 6 people.

1 whole best end of neck (12 cutlets) ✦ a piece of back pork fat sufficient to surround the roast

Get the butcher to chine the meat. Bend it round to form a crown and stitch the two ends together with coarse thread. Wrap the pork fat round and tie with string. Scrape the meat from the ends of the bones.

2 shallots ✦ 1 tablespoon butter ✦ 6 oz minced veal 1 tablespoon chopped parsley

Soften the chopped shallots in butter. Add the veal and herbs and the meat scraped from between the bones, mix well and continue cooking for a few minutes. Fill the centre of the crown with this mixture. Cover the tips of the bones with foil to prevent them burning. Roast for ½ hour in a fairly hot oven (400° F, 200 ° C, Gas 6).

Decorate the tips of the bones with cutlet frills (p. 89).

Shoulder of Mutton or Lamb Stuffed with Olives

Moderately Expensive

This dish, which is excellent cold, will serve 6 people.

2 slices bread ✦ 1 tablespoon white wine

Soak the bread in wine, squeeze it dry, and crumble it into a bowl.

8 stoned black olives 4 oz streaky bacon ✦ 1 egg 8 oz minced veal ✦ 2 crushed cloves garlic chopped parsley and chervil (1 tablespoon) salt, pepper ✦ a pinch nutmeg

Chop the olives and bacon, and mix them with the bread and the rest of the ingredients.

2 lb boned shoulder
1 tablespoon lard or fat

Stuff the meat, roll and tie it. Brown it all over in a flameproof casserole.

4 tomatoes ✦ 2 cloves garlic ✦ ½ glass white wine (or stock) ✦ salt and pepper ✦ a bay leaf

Chop the flesh of the tomatoes with the garlic and arrange it round the meat, adding the wine and seasoning.

Put the lid on the casserole and simmer for 2 to 3 hours, turning the meat from time to time. Add a little wine if the sauce becomes too thick. Remove the bay leaf. Decorate the meat with black olives and serve with French beans.

Stuffed Shoulder Bonne Femme Economical

This will serve 6 people.

2 lb boned shoulder of mutton ✦ ½ lb sausage meat ✦ 1 tablespoon chopped parsley ✦ salt and pepper

Make a stuffing with the sausage meat and parsley, well seasoned. Roll it up in the meat, and tie.

6 oz salt streaky pork ✦ 8 large potatoes ✦ 4 onions salt and pepper ✦ 2 tablespoons fat

Brown the diced pork. Slice the potatoes and onions finely. Mix all together, season, and put them into a buttered fireproof dish. Place the stuffed shoulder on top and brush it with melted fat.

Put the meat in a very hot oven (445° F, 230° C, Gas 8) turning it after 5 minutes, and basting. When it is browned (about 10 minutes more) reduce the heat to 380° F, 195° C, Gas 5). Cook for ½ hour, basting frequently. Remove unwanted fat, and serve.

Shashliks Economical

Shashliks are a Russian speciality rather similar to shish kebabs. They are made with mutton or beef and cooked on a spit (or sword) over an open fire.

1¼ lb boned shoulder of mutton ✦ 1 tablespoon oil ✦ 1 teaspoon honey
4 onions cut in rings
½ glass vinegar
1 teaspoon thyme

Cut the meat in pieces, brush them lightly with honey, sprinkle with oil and put them with the sliced onion rings to marinate in vinegar for 3–4 hours.

Drain the meat well and thread it on the spit alternately with onion rings. Sprinkle with thyme and grill for 20 minutes over an open fire, turning frequently and being careful to keep the meat away from any flame.

Shoulder or neck of lamb prepared in this way are excellent.

Shish Kebab Economical

This dish, of Turkish or Greek origin, is made with small pieces of mutton, lamb or sometimes veal on skewers. Use shoulder of mutton or neck of lamb.

1¼ lb meat ✦ salt and pepper ✦ 1 teaspoon thyme ✦ a pinch powdered bay leaf ✦ 2 glasses milk	Cut the meat in small pieces and rub them all over with salt and pepper, crushed thyme and bay leaf. Marinate in milk for 4 hours, then drain and dry in a cloth.
4 tomatoes ✦ 4 green peppers ✦ 4 onions	Slice the tomatoes fairly thickly, removing the pips. Halve the peppers and scoop out the seeds. Cut them into squares. Slice the onions in rings.
4 bay leaves	Thread the skewers with meat and vegetables alternately, putting a bay leaf in the centre of each. Grill over a hot fire, turning frequently.

Serve with rice and spring onions.

Roast Sucking Lamb Expensive

If your oven is not big enough to take the whole lamb cut it in half.

4 to 6 cloves garlic ✦ salt and pepper ✦ thyme	Insert pieces of garlic here and there in the meat, and season it generously.
1–2 tablespoons strong French mustard ✦ 5 or 6 tablespoons oil	Spread the lamb with mustard, and oil it copiously.
10 potatoes ✦ salt and pepper	Peel and slice the potatoes and put them into a greased baking tin. Season. Place the lamb, breast down, on the potatoes, and put the dish into an oven pre-heated to 425° F (220° C, Gas 7). Cook for ¾ hour, turn the meat over and cook for another ½ hour at 355° F (180° C, Gas 4) without basting.

You can mix slices of onion with the potatoes.

Sucking Lamb Stuffed Expensive

This is enough for 8 people. Use the hindquarter of the lamb, including the kidney and liver.

3 large onions ✦ 3 tablespoons butter ✦ the lamb's liver and kidneys ✦ 4 sprigs parsley	Chop the onions and let them soften in the butter for 10 minutes, without taking colour. Chop the liver and kidneys with the parsley.
2 eggs ✦ 1½ tablespoons brandy (optional) ✦ salt and pepper	Mix all the ingredients together with the eggs and brandy. Season.
thyme ✦ 2 tablespoons oil a piece caul fat	Brush the inside of the lamb with oil and sprinkle it with thyme, salt and pepper. Fill it with stuffing and cover this with caul fat. Fold the skin of the flanks round and sew it together.
4 cloves garlic ✦ 4 tablespoons oil	Insert pieces of garlic into the meat, and brush it abundantly with oil.
8–10 potatoes ✦ salt and pepper	Peel the potatoes and cut them in slices. Put the lamb, breast up, on a bed of potatoes and cook ¾ hour at 445° F (230° C, Gas 8). Reduce the heat to 355° F (180° C, Gas 4) and roast for a further ¾ hour.

Chops and Cutlets

There are three types of chops; chump, loin and those from the best end of the neck which are usually referred to as cutlets.

Chump chops, which are taken from the leg end of the loin, are compact and meaty with only a small piece of bone in the centre.

Loin chops have a small T-bone and contain less meat than chump chops. They are, however, more delicate in flavour and texture. Both of these chops, when grilled, are usually cut about an inch thick.

Cutlets. The best end of neck, which consists of five or six pairs of ribs, can be divided into cutlets. These have curved bones. Some butchers chop the backbone, leaving an awkward piece of bone which spoils the appearance of the cutlets. Unless your butcher is skilful it is best to ask him to chine the meat (saw through the split backbone) so that you can remove it and divide the cutlets yourself.

To prepare chops and cutlets. Both chops and cutlets should be neatly trimmed to remove all skin and superfluous fat, and flattened with a cutlet bat or rolling pin.

A well-browned outside adds very much to the flavour of a chop, but if you like the inside well done, see that the chop is not cut too thick, otherwise the outside will burn before the inside is ready.

If the chops are to be grilled, which is the best way of cooking them, brush them with oil half an hour beforehand. If you like the centre of your chop to be juicy, turn it over as soon as beads of liquid form on the surface, being sure not to pierce the meat and allow the juice to run out. Do not salt the chops until they are ready.

If you are sautéing chops or cutlets heat a small quantity of oil or butter until smoke just begins to rise. (Unless the fat is really hot the meat will be saturated with grease and the juice will escape.) Put the meat in the pan, being sure that each piece lies flat. Turn the chops when they are brown, being careful not to pierce the surfaces. When the meat looks puffy and is slightly resistant to the touch it is done.

How to serve chops and cutlets. These are excellent accompanied by chipped or straw potatoes, watercress, tomatoes, grilled mushrooms, French beans and a pat of fresh, or *maître d'hôtel*, butter.

Marinaded Mutton Chops Moderately expensive

This recipe is excellent for more elderly meat.

1 glass white wine ✦ ½ glass vinegar ✦ 1 onion 2 cloves ✦ 1 carrot ✦ 1 stalk celery ✦ 6 peppercorns ✦ a bouquet garni	Bring all the ingredients to the boil and simmer for 15 minutes in a small saucepan. Let them cool.
4 mutton chops ✦ 2 tablespoons oil ✦ salt and pepper ✦ juice of ½ lemon	Season the chops and dip them in oil and lemon juice. Cover them with the marinade and leave them in a cool place for from 24–48 hours, turning occasionally.
1 tablespoon honey	Drain and dry the chops and brush

1 tablespoon oil	them with honey. Heat the oil to smoking point and brown the chops all over.
1 teaspoon cornflour	Mix the cornflour with a little cold water. Stir it into the marinade and cook for a minute or two. Strain the sauce and pour it over the meat, heating for 5 minutes more.

Lamb and Mutton Ragoûts, or Stews

Ragoûts, or stews, of mutton and lamb are very economical and become even more so if you increase the proportion of cheaper vegetables used in making them.

Choosing the meat. Shoulder, middle neck, scrag and breast are all suitable for stews and ragoûts. These cuts vary in price and in the amount of bone and fat which they contain. By mixing, for instance, scrag and breast, one can modify the character of a dish and pay slightly more or less, as one wishes.

Middle neck is an excellent cheap cut and makes very good stews.

You should allow about 6–8 oz of boneless meat for each person and about 8–10 oz with bone.

Preparation. Mutton is much improved by being well browned before any liquid is added. It is best to put only a limited number of pieces of meat in the pan at a time, and to use as little extra fat as possible to brown them, since the meat itself will have plenty of fat.

The stew will be more pleasant to eat if, before serving, you remove the bone.

To serve. As we have already mentioned, mutton, with its pronounced flavour, should be accompanied by vegetables with a decided taste such as turnips, onions, leeks and, if one can find it, celeriac. Lamb would be overpowered by these strong flavours and should be served with delicate spring vegetables, or French beans, young green peas, button onions, etc.

And remember, please—hot plates!

Blanquette of Lamb Economical

about 2 lb breast or neck of lamb	Cut the meat in regular pieces. After removing excess fat let it soak in cold water for ½ hour. Drain and dry. Put the lamb in a flameproof casserole covered with cold water. Bring to the boil and skim.
1 onion ✦ 2 cloves ✦ 1 carrot ✦ a bouquet garni peel of 1 lemon ✦ a stalk celery ✦ 3 or 4 cloves garlic ✦ salt and pepper	Cut the vegetables in large pieces and add them, with seasoning and herbs, to the casserole. Simmer ¾ hour. Lift out the meat and drain it.
6 oz ham ✦ 2 tablespoons butter ✦ 2 tablespoons flour	Chop the ham coarsely, warm it in the butter, sprinkle with flour and stir in 2½ glasses of the liquid from the casserole, taking care that no lumps are formed. Cook gently for 10 minutes. Add the meat and heat it through.
2 yolks egg ✦ 3 tablespoons cream	Mix the egg yolks and cream in a bowl. Whisk in, a little at a time, a glass of very hot liquid from the meat. Pour the mixture back into the casserole, whisking all the time. Watch that it does not boil.
juice of ½ lemon ✦ 1 teaspoon minced parsley ✦ a pinch cayenne pepper	Stir these into the sauce and serve.

Ragoût of Lamb a l'Italienne Economical

about 2 lb lamb ✦ 1 teaspoon lard or fat	Cut the lamb in large pieces. Heat the fat in a frying pan. Brown the meat and then pour off the fat from the pan.
6 anchovy fillets ✦ 2 cloves garlic ✦ 1 teaspoon grated lemon rind ✦ pepper ✦ 2 tablespoons wine vinegar	Crush the anchovies with a fork, mix them with the crushed garlic, flavourings and vinegar, and pour into the frying pan.

1 tablespoon flour ✦ 1 glass hot bouillon or water	Dredge with flour and add the hot liquid a little at a time. Cover the pan and cook for ¾ hour stirring frequently.

Casserole of Lamb and Potatoes Economical

about 2 lb lamb ✦ 2 tablespoons flour ✦ salt and pepper	Cut the meat in 1½-inch squares. Season, and roll in flour.
1 tablespoon lard or fat	Make the fat smoking hot and brown the meat. Lift it out and put it in a casserole.
4 potatoes ✦ 4 onions ✦ salt and pepper ✦ ¼ teaspoon powdered ginger ✦ juice of ½ lemon ✦ ½ glass bouillon	Arrange the potatoes and onions, peeled and sliced, round the meat. Season, sprinkle with lemon juice, add the hot bouillon, cover and cook in a moderate oven (355° F, 180 °C, Gas 4) for 1½ hours.

Ragoût d'Agneau Printanière Economical

4 oz salt streaky pork ✦ 1 onion ✦ 1 tablespoon fat	Brown the diced pork and chopped onion in a casserole.
about 2 lb middle neck of lamb ✦ salt and pepper 2 tablespoons flour 1 glass white wine *or* stock	Cut the meat in regular pieces, removing excess fat. Brown it in the casserole and season. Dredge with flour and stir in the wine, avoiding lumps.
1 glass bouillon ✦ 3 tablespoons tomato purée ✦ 3 or 4 cloves garlic	Mix the tomato purée with hot bouillon and add to the casserole together with the garlic, chopped coarsely.
onions ✦ young carrots and turnips (about 8 of each)	Blanch the carrots and turnips in boiling, salted water for 5 minutes, drain and drop them into the casserole for 10 minutes' gentle cooking.
½ lb French beans ✦ 1 cup fresh peas (blanched in boiling water) ✦ 2 tablespoons chopped, mixed chervil, parsley and chives salt and pepper ✦ 2 tablespoons butter	Remove the surplus fat and add the peas, beans and herbs, and stir. Cook all together for a few minutes. Season and serve, topped with fresh butter.

Navarin of Mutton Economical

about 2 lb mutton ✦ 1 teaspoon lard or fat ✦ 2 tablespoons flour	Cut the meat in fairly large pieces, brown them, sprinkle with flour and let this colour too.
4 cloves garlic ✦ 3 tablespoons tomato purée ✦ 2 glasses water ✦ salt and pepper ✦ a bouquet garni	Add the tomato purée, herbs, seasoning and hot water and simmer for 1 hour. Remove the bouquet.
4 onions ✦ 4 carrots ✦ 4 turnips ✦ ⅓ celeriac root	Brown the sliced vegetables in a little fat and let them cook for ½ hour more in the casserole.
8 potatoes ✦ salt and pepper	Cut the potatoes in large pieces and cook them with the rest for another ½ hour. Season. Remove surplus fat, and serve.

Stewed Mutton with Haricot Beans Very economical

* 10–12 oz cooked haricot beans ✦ 2 tablespoons butter ✦ 4 tomatoes ✦ 2 or 3 cloves garlic ✦ 3 tablespoons tomato purée ✦ 2 glasses bouillon ✦ salt and pepper ✦ a bouquet garni	Brown the haricot beans in butter. Chop the flesh of the tomatoes and put them with the garlic, tomato purée mixed with bouillon, herbs and seasoning and the beans, into a flameproof casserole and cook for 10 minutes.
6 oz diced bacon ✦ 1¾ lb stewing mutton	Brown the bacon and the meat, cut into 1-inch squares, in a frying pan. Dredge with flour, let this colour and add the meat and bacon to the casserole. Simmer for ½ hour, stirring to avoid burning, taking care not to break the beans. Remove the bouquet and surplus fat.

* Soak the beans for several hours in cold water, then cook them for 2 hours in unsalted water. Drain and cool.

Stewed Mutton with Broad Beans Very economical

This dish is only good if the beans are very young, and care must be taken to remove any stringy bits. The beans, with their pods, should be cut in regular pieces.

Use half breast and half neck of mutton.

4 onions ✦ 1 teaspoon lard or fat ✦ $1\frac{3}{4}$ lb meat ✦ 2 tablespoons flour
1 lb young broad beans
3 glasses hot water

Brown the chopped onions and with them the meat, cut in $1\frac{1}{2}$-inch pieces. Dredge with flour and let this colour. Add the sliced beans and hot water. Cover the pan and cook very gently for $2\frac{1}{2}$ hours.

4 tomatoes ✦ 2 or 3 cloves garlic ✦ salt and pepper

Remove the skin and pips from the tomatoes. Chop them with the garlic and add them to the meat. Season, and simmer 1 hour.

Haricot de Mouton Very economical

Strangely enough, this stew has nothing to do with haricot beans. Its name comes from the verb '*halicoter*' which means to cut in little pieces.

$1\frac{3}{4}$ lb stewing mutton ✦ 1 onion ✦ 1 tablespoon lard
$\frac{1}{2}$ teaspoon sugar ✦ 2 tablespoons flour ✦ 3 cloves garlic

Brown, in a flameproof casserole, the sliced onions and the mutton, cut in pieces. Sprinkle them with flour, sugar and chopped garlic, and stir well.

3 glasses hot water ✦ 3 tablespoons tomato purée
a bouquet garni

Dissolve the tomato purée in hot water and pour it into the casserole. Add the bouquet garni. Close the lid and simmer for 1 hour. Remove the bones and surplus fat from the meat.

8–10 potatoes ✦ 4 onions
4 turnips

Cut the vegetables in large pieces and cook them, together with the meat, for 1 hour more. Skim off unwanted fat and serve.

Cassoulet of Mutton and Pork Very economical

3 cups dried haricot beans

Soak the beans in cold water for 3 hours. Drain and bring them to the boil in fresh, unsalted cold water. Simmer $1\frac{1}{2}$ hours.

1 lb boned shoulder of mutton ✦ 8 oz lean pork
4 oz streaky bacon ✦ 1 tablespoon lard or fat
6–8 cloves garlic, crushed

Cut the mutton in large pieces and the pork and bacon in dice. Brown them all in a saucepan. Add the crushed garlic and after a moment or two, the beans.

3 tablespoons tomato purée ✦ 3 or 4 glasses hot water ✦ salt and pepper	Dilute the tomato purée and pour it into the saucepan with enough water to cover the meat. Simmer for 2 hours, adding more hot water if necessary.
6 oz garlic sausage	Cut the sausage in thick slices and let it cook, in the casserole, for 1½ hours.
½ lb pure pork sausages 1 teaspoon fat	Prick the sausages here and there with a needle. Fry them with very little fat and lift on to a plate. Cut them in large pieces.
4–5 tomatoes ✦ 1 tablespoon tomato purée ✦ salt and pepper	Chop the flesh of the tomatoes and heat it gently in the sausage pan. Add the tomato purée, cover and simmer for ½ hour. Season abundantly and strain. Put the meat, beans, and sausages into a fireproof dish with the tomato sauce. Brown in the oven for ½ hour.

Irish Stew

In France, this may be considered an exciting foreign dish. Here, it is only too well known, so we will leave those who cook it well to follow their own excellent recipes.

A Good Curry Economical

This is curry with a French accent. You can make it with any kind of meat, or chicken, on top of the stove or in the oven. If you do not like strong curry, add the powder with caution, tasting as you go, but remember that the flavour will be softened by the cream.

2 or 3 onions ✦ 3 cloves garlic ✦ 2 tomatoes ✦ 2 stalks celery ✦ 1 apple 2 green peppers (optional)	Slice the onions. Halve each garlic clove. Chop the tomato flesh and the celery. Cut the peeled apple in small pieces. Remove the seeds from the peppers and slice them finely.
peel of 1 orange ✦ ¼ small red pepper (optional) ✦ 2 tablespoons fat	Heat the fat and allow all the ingredients to soften in it. (The red pepper is only for those who enjoy very hot dishes.)
2 tablespoons flour about 2 tablespoons curry powder ✦ 1 glass stock or water	Sprinkle with flour and curry powder. Stir over a low fire for 15 minutes. Add the stock and cook very gently for 2 hours.

½ cup raisins ✦ 2 bananas 2 hard-boiled eggs (optional) ✦ 2 tablespoons grated coconut	Meanwhile, soak the raisins in water for 1 hour. Dry them and add them with the sliced bananas, eggs and coconut to the curry.
3 or 4 tablespoons fresh cream	Just before serving, remove any surplus fat and stir in the cream.

Mousaka in a Mould Very economical

Mousaka is eaten in Greece, Turkey and Roumania.

It is usually made with mutton, though beef and veal can be used instead. It is generally baked in a fireproof dish with meat and aubergines in alternate layers, but it is also excellent cooked in a mould lined with aubergines, as we shall describe.

4 aubergines	Cut the aubergines in half lengthwise, rub them with coarse salt and, after 15 minutes, dry off the juice which has oozed out.
4 tablespoons oil	Heat the oil in a frying pan and cook the aubergines gently. Drain them and scoop out the flesh without breaking the skins. Line a buttered mould with the skins, purple side out.
* 1 lb minced neck or shoulder of mutton ✦ 2 onions ✦ 3 tablespoons tomato purée ✦ 2 cloves garlic, crushed ✦ 1 teaspoon minced parsley	Mix everything together with the flesh of the aubergines and cook gently for 10 minutes.
2 egg yolks	Lift the pan from the fire and stir in the egg yolks. Fill the mould, pressing the mixture in well. Cover it with greased paper or foil. Cook in a bain-marie or in the oven for ¾ hour. Let it rest for 4-5 minutes before turning out the mould. Serve with a very spicy tomato sauce.

* Remains of braised meat are excellent for this dish.

USUAL CUTS OF PORK IN LONDON AND THE HOME COUNTIES

Cut	Position	Characteristics	Cooking Suggestions
Leg	Hind leg of animal.	Being rather a large joint it is sometimes cut in two. Sold whole, it is moderate in price. Boned, and without the knuckle, it costs about the same as loin.	If roasted, the skin should be scored by the butcher to make crackling. It may also be salted and boiled.
Fillet	As with veal and lamb this name is generally used for the upper part of the back leg.	An expensive cut with minimum waste.	Slices of fillet are excellent grilled or fried.
Tenderloin	Corresponds to the fillet of beef.	Tenderloin is not used in bacon manufacture but cut from the carcase and sold wholesale to butchers. Like beef fillet, it is very tender and there is no waste.	Excellent for roasting or grilling.
Loin		Good roasting joint expensive when boned. It is sometimes divided into hind and fore loin, each with half the kidney.	Makes a good roast, either boned and rolled or on the bone.

Cut	Position	Characteristics	Cooking Suggestions
Chops		Chump chops with a compact meaty centre, and loin chops with an eye of meat and often a piece of kidney, are cut from the hind loin. Chops from the fore loin have lean and fat interspersed.	Pork chops are excellent grilled or fried provided surplus fat is trimmed off before cooking.
Short Ribs	The lower part of the loin ribs.	When the loin is boned, the lower part of the ribs, or short ribs, are left with the meat on them and sold separately.	This is a popular cut for a barbecue.
Blade Bone	The top of the fore leg.	A tender joint reasonably priced.	Excellent boned, stuffed, and then roasted or braised.
Spare Ribs	The part immediately behind the head which is left when the blade and hand have been removed.	Medium-priced and fairly lean joint. It can be divided into cutlets.	May be roasted, braised, stewed or barbecued.
Shoulder (including Blade and Spare Ribs)	Shoulder and front leg of the animal.	Some butchers sell shoulder with the bone removed. This can be rolled and cut to the required size. The fatter jowl end is cheaper than the fillet end.	Roast or braise.

PORK (continued)

Cut	Position	Characteristics	Cooking Suggestions
Hand and Spring	The fore leg of the animal.	A cheap cut, but rather large. It has a sweet and nutty flavour. The knuckle can be removed and salted and the rest boned and rolled.	Rolled and boned the hand makes an economical roasting joint, especially if stuffed. The knuckle, after salting, can be boiled.
Belly (or Streaky)		A cheap cut, but rather fat. The thicker end is firm and cushiony, and the thinner is often sliced into rashers.	Usually salted and boiled. The thicker end may be rolled and roasted and the thinner end, cut in slices, is excellent grilled or fried.
Head		Reaches the butcher attached to the carcase. Pig's cheek is sometimes sold separately. It is also used to make Bath Chaps. Pig's head is cheap.	Generally used to make brawn. The cheek may be breadcrumbed and baked. The ears are sometimes stuffed and braised or fricasseed, or set in a jelly with the feet.
Tongue		Usually sold fresh, but may be salted.	If fresh, usually boiled and served hot with sauce. If salted, pigs' tongues are eaten cold and are best pressed into a round with jelly.
Feet (or Trotters)		Very cheap. These are often sold cooked. Pigs' feet make a good substitute for calves' feet or fresh pork rind in dishes such as *bœuf à la mode*.	

PORK

THE pig, like the elephant, is a pachyderm or thick-skinned animal. Useless during its life, which is usually only a short one, the pig once dead is a valuable creature. Most of him, from snout to tail, can be eaten; his bristles are made into brushes, the softer hair into stuffing for upholstery, and his thick skin is transformed into smart gloves and elegant luggage.

In many countries where oxen are used for work in the fields their meat is tough and so pork is preferred. Both the Moslem and the Jewish religions, however, prohibit the use of pork. This was originally on the grounds of hygiene since in hot climates pigs are subject to disease and their flesh also decomposes rapidly.

Pigs have always been popular in France and in the twelfth century these animals running loose in the streets of Paris caused so many accidents that it was forbidden to keep them in the city. An exception was made for those belonging to the Abbey of St. Antoine, which had to wear bells round their necks. Any pig found wandering without a bell—like the cats in Gibraltar during the war—was put to death.

Pigs fatten very rapidly and in France they weigh an average of 220 lb when slaughtered. Largely owing to the public aversion to fat great efforts have been made in this country to breed leaner pigs, and our porkers seldom weigh more than 100 lb when they are killed. The thinner layer of fat beneath the rind of English pork makes delicious crackling—a thing which is almost unknown in France where the rind is sold separately and part of the thick layer of fat beneath it is removed to make bards for lean meat. Most English butchers sell fresh or salt rind of pork, which is trimmed off before chops are cut, and this is a most useful addition to a braise.

It used to be considered unsafe to eat pork in warm weather, but provided it is kept refrigerated pork can now be eaten all the year round, though it is best when the weather is cool.

Pork is really red meat, and only becomes pale after it has been bled. It is less digestible than beef or mutton but more easily assimilated, and it contains Vitamin B1 which tones the nerves and combats fatigue, insomnia and cramp. Doctors do not advise it for those who are trying to slim, or in the case of certain liver complaints.

How to buy pork. Choose, if possible, meat from a smaller animal. The lean should be pale pink, smooth and finely grained; the fat, white and firm. If the lean is too pale the animal has been poorly fed; if too dark, it will be dry and tough. Avoid any reddish tinge in the lean or the least sign of enlarged glands. Pork should have no smell.

Unlike beef, which is best when it is marbled and has a generous proportion of fat, pork should not be too fatty. The meat will have more flavour if it is cooked on the bone.

Allow 6–7 oz of meat without bone for each person, and from 8–12 oz in the case of cuts with bone.

To cook pork. Pork should never be underdone. In order to make it more digestible the surplus fat should be removed, and the meat will be more tender if it is cooked at a moderate temperature (30–35 minutes to the lb at 380° F, 195° C, Gas 5).

Unlike beef, pork should be seasoned before cooking.

Pickled pork is usually boiled for 25–30 minutes to the pound and 30 minutes over.

How to serve it. Since pork is by its nature more suitable for a winter dish, it tends to be accompanied by the heavier

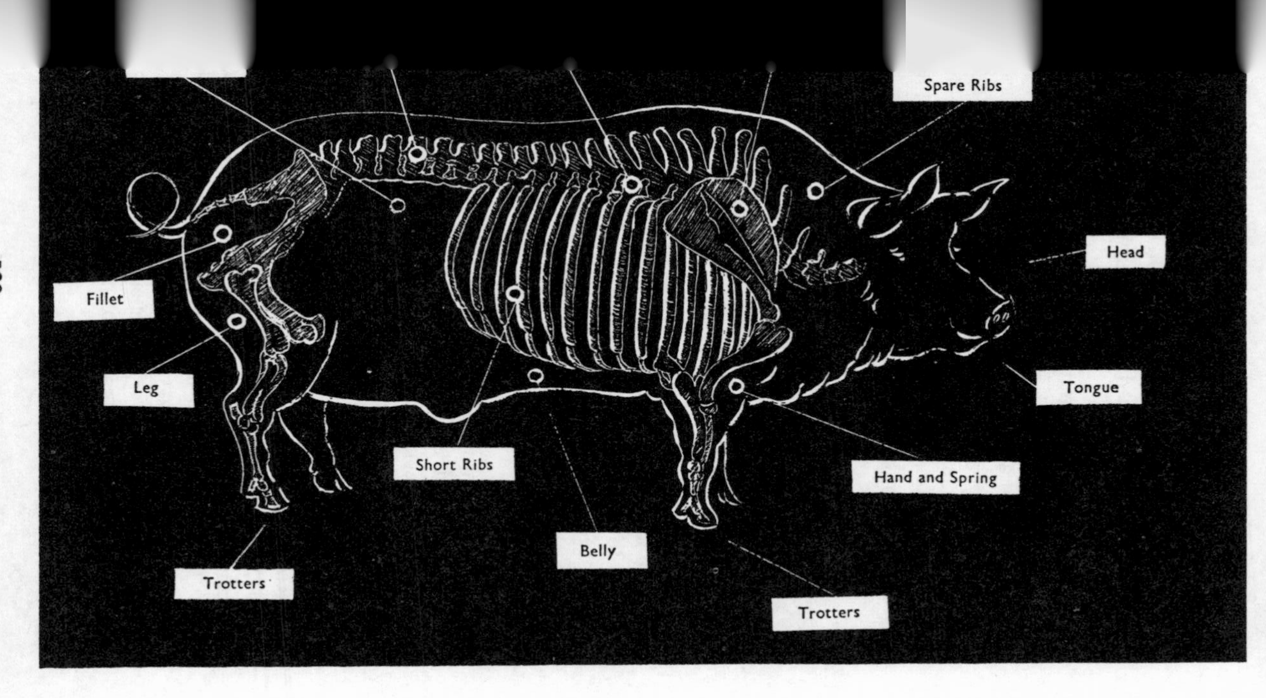

Spare Ribs
Head
Tongue
Hand and Spring
Trotters
Belly
Short Ribs
Fillet
Leg
Trotters

vegetables such as cabbage, Brussels sprouts and choucroûte, and of course plain boiled potatoes. It is, however, excellent with chicory, braised celery, turnips, carrots, French beans, tomatoes or lentils.

Pork, being fat and rather rich, demands a refreshing contrast like the traditional English apple sauce, or apples baked in the oven and sharpened with lemon rind. In some parts of France gooseberry jelly is eaten with pork, and the Americans use tart cranberry sauce, grilled apricots or pickled peaches. Pineapple, oranges, honey, soya and bamboo shoots as used in China and Hawaii, blend very well with pork.

Sucking Pig

This can be ordered from some butchers. The pig will probably be between 3 and 4 weeks old and will weigh between 8 and 15 lb. It should be cooked as soon as possible after it is killed.

Before roasting, clean the pig carefully. Season it well, fill it with a stuffing perfumed with herbs, lemon, cognac, etc. and sew it up. Brush the surface with oil, sprinkle it with salt, and roast for 35 minutes to the lb at 355° F (180° C, Gas 4) basting frequently. About 15 minutes before it is ready sprinkle with flour to make a beautiful brown crust and raise the heat a little, if necessary.

If the joint is too big for your oven ask the butcher to cut it in half, and cook the hind and forequarter with different accompaniments. The large classic cookery books describe wonderful sauces and garnishes for sucking pig, and you can adapt many of the ideas suggested in this book for pork.

Roasts and Braises

All cuts of pork, provided they are tender and fairly fat, can be roasted.

Cutlets from the fore-loin may be used to make a crown roast in the same way as lamb (p. 112). This is an impressive dish which is not very expensive.

There are various ways of marinading and seasoning pork. Here are some of them:

A few hours before cooking:

Rub the meat with aromatic herbs, salt, pepper and crushed garlic.

Make small slits in the meat and insert slivers of garlic, sage or some cloves, being careful that no ends protrude as they may burn.

Brush the joint with olive oil and white wine, or wine vinegar. Since vinegar has a strong flavour, about 1 tablespoonful for each pound of meat is sufficient. (The flavour of the vinegar will be much improved if you first simmer it with a little brown sugar.) You can be more generous with wine. If you wish to economize, substitute plain water.

Before putting the meat in the oven:

Rub it with caster sugar, honey, moist brown sugar, mustard or even jam. The fragrance of honey goes particularly well with pork and it will give the meat a marvellous golden crust.

Put the seasoned meat on an oven dish fat-side uppermost. It is not usually necessary to add extra fat.

Cooking:

Pork should be cooked in a moderate oven at about 380° F (195° C, Gas 5) for 30–35 minutes to the lb.

If you like crisp crackling, score the meat across with a sharp knife (or get the butcher to do this for you) and stand the meat on a rack. Rub the outside with olive oil or dripping.

During roasting you can add to the flavour of the joint by basting it with vinegar or white wine, tomato, pineapple or orange juice, soya extract or cider.

Marinaded Pork Moderately expensive

about 2 lb leg of pork ✦ 3 or 4 glasses white wine ✦ 1 carrot ✦ 1 onion or 2 shallots ✦ a stalk celery ✦ a bouquet garni ✦ 8 peppercorns

Slice the vegetables and put them with the wine, herbs and pork into a deep dish. Marinate for 8 hours, turning the meat from time to time. Lift out the meat, drain it and wipe it dry.

Simmer the marinade for ½ hour.

First method. (Particularly suitable for the knuckle end of leg)

salt and pepper ✦ 1 tablespoon flour ✦ 1 tablespoon fat	Rub the meat with salt and pepper and sprinkle it with flour. Heat the fat in a flameproof casserole. Brown the meat all over and add the strained marinade, little by little. Cook gently with the lid off for 45 minutes. Lift the meat on to a lightly greased fireproof dish.
4 tablespoons breadcrumbs ✦ 2 tablespoons melted butter	Sprinkle the pork with breadcrumbs and melted butter and brown in a hot oven (425° F, 220° C, Gas 7) for 10 minutes. Let the sauce bubble for a few moments and serve it separately.

Second method

Meat and marinade as before

1 tablespoon honey ✦ salt and pepper ✦ ½ teaspoon thyme	Rub the meat with salt and pepper, brush it with honey and sprinkle with thyme. Brown it in a hot oven (425° F, 220° C, Gas 7) for 15 minutes. Reduce the heat to 355° F (180° C, Gas 4) and cook the pork for 40–45 minutes more, basting every 5 minutes with a little strained marinade. Remove any surplus fat from the sauce.

Roast Pork with Turnips Economical

about 2 lb pork ✦ ½ teaspoon lard ✦ salt and pepper ✦ 2 teaspoons caster sugar ✦ 3 tablespoons bouillon	Rub the meat with seasoning, sprinkle it with sugar, and roast it on a fireproof dish greased with lard, according to the second method described above, basting it from time to time with bouillon.
12 small turnips, or 4 larger ones cut and shaped like small ones ✦ 2 tablespoons fat ✦ 1 teaspoon sugar ✦ salt and pepper 4 tablespoons bouillon	Meanwhile, brown the turnips in a saucepan. Sprinkle them with sugar and seasoning. Add the bouillon, cover and simmer for 15 minutes. Arrange them round the meat ½ hour before it leaves the oven. Remove all surplus fat before serving.

Pork with Capers Economical

about 2 lb boned pork ✦ 1 onion ✦ 1 carrot ✦ 1 clove garlic ✦ a bouquet garni 6 peppercorns ✦ 2 glasses red wine

Chop the vegetables finely and put them with the herbs, peppercorns and meat into a deep dish. Pour in the wine, and marinate for at least 8 hours. Lift out the meat, drain and dry it. Let the marinade reduce a little over a low fire.

2 tablespoons butter ✦ 1 tablespoon flour ✦ ½ glass bouillon ✦ salt and pepper

Heat the butter in a flameproof casserole and brown the pork all over. Dust with flour and add, gradually, the strained marinade and hot bouillon. Bring to the boil. Put on the lid and simmer for 2 hours. Lift out the meat and cut it in fine slices. Meanwhile, reduce the sauce over a gentle fire.

2 or 3 tablespoons capers

At the last moment, add the capers to the sauce. Pour it over the meat, and serve.

Pork Stewed in Milk Economical

This is an Italian dish which is not easy to make, but so delicious that it is really worth trying.

Choose a casserole which is not too big, as the milk, without being too abundant, must cover the pork.

about 2 lb pork ✦ salt and pepper ✦ 1 clove garlic ✦ 1 tablespoon fat

Insert small pieces of garlic into the pork, which you have first rubbed with salt and pepper. Brown it all over in a flameproof casserole.

2 onions ✦ 3 slices ham about 1½ pints milk

Chop the onions and ham finely and let them colour with the meat. Cover with boiling milk to about ½-inch above the surface of the meat. Lower the heat and cook gently with the lid off for 1 hour. The milk will form a brown skin clinging to the sides of the pan. Now break the skin, turn the meat and cook it for another ½ hour by which time the sauce should be reduced to about a cupful.

1 teaspoon flour ✦ 1 tablespoon butter	If the sauce is too thin, work the flour and butter together with a little liquid from the casserole and stir the mixture back into the sauce, taking care that it does not boil. Cook 5 minutes more. Serve with potato purée.

Pork with Chestnuts Economical

about 2 lb pork ✦ 1 tablespoon lard ✦ 2 stalks celery 6 small onions ✦ 2 cloves garlic ✦ 1 carrot ✦ a bouquet garni ✦ salt and pepper	Brown first the meat and then the whole vegetables in the same pan. Season.
½ glass white wine 1 glass hot water	Simmer very gently, with the wine and water, for ½ hour.
12–15 chestnuts ✦ salt and pepper ✦ a pinch sugar	Peel the chestnuts* and arrange them round the meat. Season. Cook for a further ¾ hour without stirring. Skim off any grease. Remove the carrots and celery and the bouquet.

* To remove the skins, put the chestnuts into cold water, bring them quickly to the boil, and then move the pan from the fire. Lift out two or three chestnuts at a time and peel them. You can also use the dried whole chestnuts which are on sale in some delicatessen shops. Soak them overnight in cold water, then bring them to the boil in fresh water and parboil for 15 minutes.

Pork Chops and Cutlets

As with mutton and lamb, there are three kinds of chops and cutlets of pork:

Chump chops from the rear end of the loin which have a compact, meaty centre.

Loin chops, with delicate flesh, but more bone.

Cutlets from the neck end of the loin with a small, sweet-flavoured 'nut' of meat surrounded by layers of fat.

There is not a great deal of difference in the prices of these.

Preparation. Pork chops and cutlets must always be well done. They should be carefully trimmed before cooking.

Grilling: choose plump chops about ¾- to 1-inch thick and trim off any unwanted fat. Grill them, turning once or twice so that while the centres are well done the meat is not burnt on the outside.

Frying: Trimmings can be melted down and the fat used to fry the chops. They will take from 7–10 minutes on each side.

Braised Pork Chops Moderately expensive

4 pork chops ✦ 1 teaspoon lard ✦ salt and pepper ✦ 1 tablespoon flour	Season the chops, dip them in flour and brown for 3 minutes on each side in lard, or fat trimmings.
½ glass white wine ✦ ½ glass bouillon ✦ a bouquet garni	Moisten with white wine and let it reduce to half, with the lid off the pan. Add the bouillon, warmed, and a bouquet garni. Replace the lid, simmer for 20 minutes, then lift out the chops and keep them hot.
½ teaspoon meat extract or some browning ✦ 1 tablespoon mixed chopped chives and parsley	Let the sauce reduce until it is creamy. Colour it with meat extract, add the herbs, pour over the meat, and serve.

Danish Pork Chops Economical

This dish is popular with most children.

12 prunes ✦ 2 apples	Soak the prunes in tepid water for 1 hour. Peel and core the apples and cut them in four.
4 pork chops ✦ 1 teaspoon lard	Brown the chops in a frying pan, using lard or trimmed-off fat. Put them in a casserole surrounded by the fruit.
1½ tablespoons flour 1 glass milk	Pour away some of the fat from the pan, dredge with flour and stir in the milk, a little at a time, taking care to avoid lumps.

½ teaspoon caster sugar
salt and pepper

Season the sauce and let it thicken over a low fire. Pour it over the fruit and meat. Close the casserole and cook in a moderate oven (380° F, 195° C, Gas 5) for 1 hour.

Pork Chops with Mustard Economical

4 pork chops ✦ 1 teaspoon lard

Heat the fat in a heavy iron casserole. Brown the chops over a hot fire, reduce the heat and continue to cook them for 5 minutes on each side.

2 shallots ✦ 2 teaspoons flour ✦ ½ glass white wine
½ glass bouillon

Lift out the meat and let the chopped shallots melt without taking colour. Dredge with flour and add the wine and bouillon gradually, stirring all the time. Reduce for 5 minutes, put back the pork chops, and continue cooking over a gentle heat for another 10 minutes, with the lid off.

2 tablespoons light French mustard

Put the chops on a hot dish and keep warm. Stir the mustard into the sauce without letting it boil. Pour over the meat and serve.

Pork Chops with Orange Juice Economical

4 pork chops ✦ 1 tablespoon lard ✦ ½ orange

Brown the chops on both sides. Arrange them in a lidded fireproof dish with a half-slice of orange on each.

1 onion ✦ 2 stalks celery
1 or 2 cloves garlic

Chop the vegetables finely, brown them in the frying pan and spread them on the chops.

½ glass orange juice ✦ 1 teaspoon vinegar ✦ a pinch thyme ✦ salt and pepper

Mix the orange juice, vinegar and seasoning and pour over the chops. Cook in a moderate oven (355° F, 180° C, Gas 4) for ¾ hour. Remove the lid and brown for another ¼ hour. Serve with steamed potatoes.

Pork Chops with Gherkins Moderately expensive

4 pork chops ✦ 1 teaspoon lard ✦ 2 tablespoons light

Rub the chops with salt and pepper, spread them with mustard on both

French mustard ✦ 2 tablespoons flour

sides and coat with flour. Brown them in smoking hot fat in a large frying pan. Cover and cook on a low fire for 5 minutes.

3 or 4 gherkins ✦ 2 tablespoons vinegar ✦ ½ glass white wine

Add the vinegar and gherkins, replacing the lid rapidly. Simmer for 20 minutes more. Lift out the meat and keep it hot. Stir in the wine, scraping the bottom of the pan well. Heat the sauce and pour it over the meat.

Stuffed Pork Chops Moderately expensive

4 pork chops ✦ 2 tablespoons olive oil ✦ 1 tablespoon chopped fresh herbs salt and pepper

Marinate the chops for an hour with oil and herbs after having rubbed them well with salt and pepper. Turn the meat frequently. Grill the chops, or fry them lightly for 4–5 minutes on each side. Let them cool.

5–6 oz pig's liver ✦ 4 oz belly of pork

Mince all the ingredients, mix well, and season.

2 cloves garlic ✦ 1 tablespoon minced herbs ✦ 4 pieces caul fat

Slit a pocket in each chop and stuff it, or spread the stuffing on top. Wrap each chop in a piece of caul fat.

1 egg ✦ 1 teaspoon water 3 tablespoons breadcrumbs ½ glass oil

Beat the egg and water lightly and brush over the chops. Coat them generously with breadcrumbs and fry, two at a time, in smoking-hot oil. When they are well browned, arrange all four chops in the pan and cook gently for 5 minutes more. Garnish with fried parsley (p. 68).

Salt Pork

Salt pork, which has been pickled in brine, is not suitable for roasting. It should be washed, or if very salty, soaked in cold water before using.

Salt pork is slightly cheaper than fresh and keeps better. It takes longer to digest than fresh meat and gives a well-fed feeling which is appreciated by manual workers and hearty eaters in general.

Cabbage, choucroûte, dried vegetables and pulses such as

haricot beans, lentils and peas all go well with salt pork, which forms the basis of a number of excellent soups and stews.

Salt Pork with Cabbage Economical

about 1½ lb salt pork pepper ✦ ¼ teaspoon thyme ✦ 2 glasses water	Rub the meat with thyme and pepper, and leave it for about an hour to absorb the flavours. Put it in a flameproof casserole. Add the water, bring to the boil, skim and cover.
1 cabbage	Wash the cabbage and cut it in eight pieces. Plunge them for a moment in boiling water and drain.
freshly milled black pepper ✦ a pinch sugar ✦ 1 teaspoon flour ✦ 1 tablespoon vinegar	Put the cabbage into the casserole and season. Mix the flour and vinegar and stir them into the liquid. Cover and simmer for ¾ hour.
5 oz sour cream	Stir in the cream without letting it boil. Serve the casserole with boiled potatoes in a separate dish.

If you should use red instead of white cabbage to make this dish, put two quartered apples into the casserole 20 minutes before it has finished cooking.

Choucroûte and Salt Pork Economical

about 1½ lb salt pork pepper	Rub the meat with pepper. Put it into a large saucepan of cold water and bring it to the boil. Skim, cover and simmer for 1 hour. Lift out the meat.
1 lb choucroûte ✦ 8 peppercorns ✦ 5–6 juniper berries wrapped with the peppercorns in muslin	Wash and drain the choucroûte. Toss it with a fork and plunge it into the water in which the pork has cooked. Add the peppercorns and juniper berries and cook gently with the lid off for 2 hours.
	Replace the meat and cook for another hour. Remove the spices. Put the choucroûte, drained, in a fireproof dish with the sliced pork on top and leave them for 10 minutes in a hot oven (425° F, 220° C, Gas 7). Serve with steamed potatoes.

Choucroûte Alsacienne Moderately expensive

If the choucroûte is fresh just wash and drain it and squeeze it gently with your hands. If it has been long in pickle you must soak it in cold water for several hours. In either case toss it with a fork so that it does not cling together.

1 tablespoon lard or goose fat (p. 31) ✦ 6 oz bacon rind ✦ 1 slice belly of pork 1 lb salt pork ✦ 2 lb choucroûte ✦ 2 onions ✦ 4 cloves ✦ 1 carrot ✦ a bouquet garni ✦ 5–6 juniper berries ✦ salt and freshly-milled pepper

Grease the bottom of a flameproof casserole and line it with bacon rinds. Blanch the belly of pork in boiling water. Stud the onion with cloves and quarter the carrots. Put everything into the casserole (the juniper berries in a muslin bag). Season.

4 oz back pork fat ✦ beef bouillon or water

Lay the back pork fat (cut in thin slices) on top of the choucroûte, and pour in liquid to the same level. Cover and bring to the boil. Simmer on top of the stove or in the oven for 4 hours, removing the pork at the end of the first hour.

4 fairly thick slices ham 4 pairs Frankfurter sausages

15 minutes before the dish is ready remove the vegetables, bouquet and juniper berries. Replace the meat, cut in slices, and add the ham and sausages. Drain the choucroûte well before bringing it to table.

Serve with boiled potatoes.

Salt Pork and Haricot Beans Economical

about 1½ lb salt pork

Cover the meat with tepid water and bring it to the boil in a large saucepan. Skim.

1 clove garlic ✦ 1 carrot 2 onions ✦ 2 stalks celery a bouquet garni ✦ 6 peppercorns ✦ 2 cloves ✦ the white part of 2 leeks

Chop the vegetables coarsely and add them to the pork. Bring to the boil once more and simmer for 1 hour.

7 oz dried haricot beans which have been soaked for 2 hours

Put the beans in a saucepan of cold water with a pinch of bicarbonate of soda and bring them slowly to the boil.

Drain, and put them to simmer for another hour with the pork.

2 tablespoons butter ✦ 2 tablespoons minced parsley ✦ 1 tablespoon lemon juice

Melt the butter in a small saucepan. Add the parsley and let it soften for 2 or 3 minutes. Sharpen with lemon juice and pour over the haricot beans.

CHARCUTERIE is a useful word which describes all sorts of sausages, pâtés and preparations of meat. We have no one word to describe all these products, and they are not, as in France, sold in special shops.

The art of *charcuterie* was understood by the ancient Romans and was well established in France in the Middle Ages. In the fifteenth century the '*chaircutiers*' in Paris were given a monopoly of the sale of pork, raw as well as cooked, and to this day pork is not sold in the ordinary French butcher's shops. There used to be a number of specialized pork butchers in this country but in the South of England, at least, very few remain.

A great deal of the *charcuterie* now sold in France is made in factories and carefully controlled and stereotyped.

Our own *charcuterie* products such as pork and beef sausages, luncheon meat, black pudding, brawn and meat pastes are not particularly exciting, but we import quantities of French, Italian, Danish, Dutch, German, Hungarian and Swiss sausages and pâtes.

Large sausages which are ready for eating are called *saucissons* by the French, whilst those which require cooking are described as *saucisses*. These are made in all sorts of sizes and usually filled with pork or beef, minced or cut up more or less finely, seasoned and mixed with such things as garlic, eggs, aromatic herbs, truffles, etc.

A description of some of these French specialities may be

useful, especially if you are shopping in Soho or travelling. There are all sorts of delicious terrines and pâtés, and in France each working *charcutier* is a real craftsman. Many of them use recipes which have been handed down in their own families.

Brawn, etc.

Hure de porc is made of whole pig's head and calf's tongue brined and cut into strips to which are added truffles and pistachio nuts.

Tête pressée and fromage de tête. Pig's head, heart and tongue cut in large pieces, cooked in white wine or court-bouillon, then chilled beneath a weight and set in their own jelly.

Rillettes de porc are made of fat and lean meat, generally pork, cooked very slowly in lard, pounded finely and put into earthenware pots which are sealed with a layer of lard. The finest *rillettes* are those of Tours which are made partly of rabbit, and those of Le Mans which are half pork and half goose.

Andouilles and andouillettes

These are large sausage skins filled with various ingredients according to the region in which they are made. Andouilles are eaten cold, cut into slices. Andouillettes, after being sliced and brushed with melted butter, are grilled or sautéd. They are eaten with potato purée.

Andouilles de Vire are made of pig's stomach cut in pieces, and strips of fat marinaded in white wine, then cooked and smoked.

Andouilles de Bretagne. Pig's intestines threaded one inside the other, dried, smoked and cooked with aromatic herbs.

Andouillettes de Troyes. These are made of calf's crow, udder and feet.

Andouillettes de Nancy are composed of belly of pork, crow of veal, mushrooms and chopped parsley.

Crépine and crépinettes

Crépine, or caul fat, is the membrane surrounding an animal's paunch. It should be plunged in hot water before using, to make it supple.

Crépinettes are all sorts of preparations of meat, stuffings, etc., wrapped in caul and then usually bathed in melted butter, breadcrumbed and cooked. The simplest resemble flattened pork sausages.

Crépinettes cendrillon are truffled and wrapped in puff pastry. They were named after *Cendrillon*, the French Cinderella, as they used to be wrapped in buttered greaseproof paper and cooked in the hot ashes.

Boudin

Boudin is a traditional Christmas dish in France. One should allow about 4 oz for each person. Whether it is baked, grilled or fried, boudin must be pierced to prevent it from bursting, and brushed with melted butter or lard. It is generally served with apple purée, fried onions and mashed potatoes.

Boudin noir, composed of pig's blood, fat pork and onions, is the equivalent of our black pudding and there are endless regional varieties.

Boudin blanc is made of lean pork, fat, eggs and milk, with the addition of liver, foie gras and truffles.

Perhaps the pleasantest way to explore *charcuterie* is to drive unhurriedly through France eating picnic lunches as you go. You may well remember the crisp French loaf, the bottle of wine and the delights of the local *charcuterie* long after your expensive dinners are forgotten.

Frankfurters in Duffle Coats Economical

1 tablespoon fat ✦ 8 Frankfurter sausages

Heat the fat in a frying pan and brown the sausages.

8 thin slices white bread*
5 tablespoons butter

Cut the crusts from the bread and roll each sausage in a slice. Sprinkle with melted butter and crisp under the grill or in the oven.

* If the bread is fresh, use a hot knife to cut it.

Provençal Sausages Economical

4 tablespoons olive oil
4 cloves garlic ✦ 1¼ lb sausages

Heat the oil in a flameproof casserole and let the garlic cook very gently for 10 minutes, then remove it. Raise the heat and brown the sausages. Lift them out and keep hot.

1 tablespoon flour ✦ 1 glass white wine ✦ ½ glass bouillon ✦ 2 tomatoes ✦ 3 tablespoons tomato purée
salt and pepper

Sprinkle the sausages with flour, stir in the wine and hot bouillon. Add the chopped flesh of the tomatoes with the tomato purée. Season and simmer for 10 minutes.

1 teaspoon minced parsley
1 clove garlic, chopped

Return the sausages to the casserole and let them simmer very gently for 10 minutes more. Sprinkle with parsley and garlic.

Gayettes de Porc Economical

This is a Provençal dish which should be eaten cold. It will serve 6–8 people.

6 oz caul fat
10 oz pig's liver ✦ 10 oz streaky 'green' bacon ✦ 2 cloves garlic ✦ 1 tablespoon fresh chopped herbs ✦ salt and pepper
2 tablespoons brandy (optional)

Cut the caul in squares of 4–5 inches. Chop all the ingredients very finely and mix them together. Divide the mixture into 8 portions and put one in the middle of each piece of caul fat. Sprinkle with very little melted lard. Roll up each *gayette*, flatten it slightly, and cook them all in a moderate oven (355° F, 180° C, Gas 4) for ½ hour.

Saucisses Chasseur Very economical

1¼ lb fresh pork sausages
2 teaspoons lard

Prick the sausages with a pin. Melt the lard in a large frying pan and brown the sausages gently, all over. Set them aside to keep hot.

2 shallots ✦ 2 tablespoons flour ✦ 1 glass bouillon 1 tablespoon tomato purée	Chop the shallots finely and brown them in the frying pan. Sprinkle with flour and let it colour. Mix the bouillon and tomato purée and stir them into the frying pan, little by little.
2 cloves garlic, crushed ✦ a bay leaf ✦ salt and pepper 12 mushrooms ✦ 1 tablespoon butter ✦ 1 teaspoon chopped parsley	Add the garlic, crumbled bay leaf and seasoning and simmer gently for 5 minutes. Meanwhile brown the sliced mushrooms in butter and put them into the sauce together with the sausages. Simmer 15 minutes, sprinkle with parsley and serve.

Sausages with Cabbage (or Cos Lettuce) Very economical

1 cabbage (or 2 Cos lettuces) ✦ 6 oz back pork fat ✦ 1 carrot ✦ 1 onion a stalk celery ✦ 1 glass bouillon	Line the bottom of a flameproof casserole with slices of pork fat and chopped vegetables. Add the cabbage (or lettuce) washed but whole, and simmer for $\frac{1}{2}$ hour moistened with bouillon.
$1\frac{1}{4}$ lb pork sausages ✦ 2 teaspoons lard	Prick the sausages, brown them in a frying pan and lift them out. Drain the cabbage, cool it and separate the leaves. Wrap each sausage in a leaf.
$\frac{1}{2}$ teaspoon curry powder or a couple of pinches of powdered ginger	Remove the vegetables and fat pork from the casserole and season the remaining juice with curry or ginger. Lay the wrapped sausages to simmer, side by side, in the liquid for 15 minutes.
$\frac{1}{2}$ teaspoon cornflour ✦ 1 tablespoon butter ✦ juice of $\frac{1}{2}$ lemon	Work butter and flour together and stir into the sauce with the lemon juice. Heat for a few minutes without boiling, and serve.

Sausages with Haricot Beans Very economical

If the beans are fairly fresh they need only be soaked for 2 hours in cold water. Drain, and bring them to the boil in salted water. (If some of the beans float on the surface add a glass of cold water.)

1¼ lb pork sausages ✦ 2 teaspoons lard ✦ 2 cups cooked haricot beans ✦ 1 or 2 cloves garlic
3 tablespoons tomato purée ✦ 1 glass bouillon salt and pepper ✦ 1 tablespoon chopped parsley

Prick the sausages and brown them in hot lard. Chop the garlic and let it colour. Add the haricot beans, seasoned, and the sausages cut in pieces.
Stir the tomato purée, diluted with bouillon, into the pan and simmer for 10 minutes. If the sauce is too thin let it reduce, with the lid off, for 5 minutes. Sprinkle with parsley and serve.

Omelette à la Creole Very economical

The rice should be boiled, if possible, the day before. See that the grains are separate.

½ lb diced bacon ✦ 3 onions, chopped

Fry the bacon until it is crisp and golden-brown and lift it into a bowl. Set aside all but 1 tablespoon of bacon fat and brown the onions gently in this.

8 eggs ✦ salt and pepper

Salt and pepper the eggs and beat them lightly with a fork. Pour them over the onions, stirring all the time. When they are cooked put them into the bowl with the bacon.

2 cups cold cooked rice ½ teaspoon soya sauce pepper

Heat the fat you have saved (adding more if necessary) and toss the rice in it. When it is hot through, add the onions, eggs and bacon. Sprinkle with the soya, stir well and adjust the seasoning.

Bacon—or Ham—Omelet Very economical

If you wish to economize, use green streaky bacon or collar instead of the more expensive gammon cut of ham. If the bacon is too salty, plunge it for a minute or two into boiling water.

½ lb bacon or ham cut in dice ✦ 8 eggs ✦ salt and pepper ✦ butter if necessary

Brown the bacon in its own fat (or the ham with a little butter). Beat the eggs lightly with a fork, adding pepper and salt with caution.
You can pour the eggs straight over the crisp bacon or ham in the pan, or stir either into the beaten eggs and return

to the fire to cook. In each case, the omelet must be 'seized' in a very hot pan, after which the heat is lowered a little.

If you like a creamy omelet, lift the sides with a fork, tilt the pan and let the egg run beneath. Fold while the centre is still runny. If you prefer it firm, like a Spanish *tortilla*, turn it and cook on both sides.

A great deal of the success of an omelet depends on the pan, which should never be washed but rubbed clean with soft paper, using a little salt as an abrasive if necessary.

Black Pudding with Apples Very economical

The black pudding sold in most shops is very cheap, though not always particularly interesting in flavour. This recipe will improve it.

2 or 3 onions ✦ a handful raisins ✦ 1 lb apples ✦ a pinch salt ✦ ample pepper
1 tablespoon sugar

Soak the raisins in tepid water for 20 minutes. Brown the sliced onions and add the drained raisins and the apples, peeled and cut in pieces. If the apples are rather dry, add 1–2 tablespoons of water. Season, stir well together and cook with the lid on over a low fire until the purée is thick but still juicy. Remove the lid and let the purée colour slightly. Pepper abundantly.

1 lb black pudding
1 tablespoon fat

Cut the black pudding into regular pieces, pricking each in several places. Heat the fat and cook the black pudding gently for 10 minutes, then raise the heat and let it brown slightly. Serve, surrounded with the apple and onion purée.

HAM, GAMMON AND BACON

HAM, properly speaking, is the leg of a pig cured and matured in all sorts of different ways, whilst gammon is cured together with the whole side of pig by a bacon process. Nowadays, shoulder and collar are often prepared in the same way as ham. These cuts are economical, but much less delicate than ham both in flavour and texture.

It is said that the curing and smoking of pigs' flesh originated in the forests of Gaul—the present-day France—and that the Gauls supplied ham to the ancient Romans. A special Ham Fair is still held regularly in Paris and in some of the larger French cities.

Nearly every region of France produces a local ham, usually called *jambon de campagne*. Many of these hams are eaten raw, as are Parma ham from Italy, which can be as delicate as smoked salmon, and the dry pungent *jamon serrano*, or mountain ham, of Spain. Mainz and Westphalian hams from Germany and the most delicate of all, Prague ham from Czechoslovakia, are also excellent raw, though they are sometimes boiled whole.

Amongst the best known of the cooking hams are:

York ham which is dry-salt cured and lightly smoked. These hams average from 16–24 lb in weight and are cut by the oyster bone and rounded off. At Christmas time a certain number of 12 lb York hams are sold. They are rather wasteful owing to the large proportion of bone.

The words 'York ham' are often loosely used, especially on the Continent, to describe cooked ham as distinct from smoked ham which is eaten raw.

Wiltshire hams are long-cut, straw coloured and mild-cured. They are the cheapest of the English hams.

Bradenham hams, which are rather small, are processed in molasses instead of brine. This 'Chippenham cure' turns the skins black and makes the meat rather red. Only a limited number of these hams are produced and they are expensive.

Suffolk sweet-cured hams are, like Bradenham hams, prepared in molasses, but by a different process. The price is similar to that of Bradenham ham.

Irish peat-cured hams are cured in much the same way as York hams, but finished with peat smoke.

Jambon de Paris (sometimes called *jambon blanc* or *jambon demi-sel*). This ham, either very lightly smoked or not at all, is similar to York ham. (The French also refer to raw leg of pork as *jambon*, which can be rather puzzling.)

Jambonneau. In France the knuckle of pork is prepared and breadcrumbed like a ham. In England this is called a foreleg or picnic ham, though it can be made from either the fore or the back leg of the pig. It is cured in brine, not smoked.

Jambon de Bayonne is salted and then smoked with aromatic herbs. It comes from Orthez in the Bayonne district. This ham can be eaten raw or used in cooking, but never boiled.

Jambon d'Ardennes is a Belgian speciality. It is dried and smoked in wood ash.

Tinned hams, especially the American and the Danish, are excellent. The larger ones can be bought by weight, machine-sliced, and make very good sandwiches. Of the tinned 'shoulder hams' the Dutch are the meatiest.

How to buy a ham. A whole ham is an expensive item and you will probably only buy it for a special occasion or for a large family. Choose a short, thick leg without too much fat. The rind should be thin and the bone fine. A useful test of the quality of a ham is to run a skewer or pointed knife in beside the bone. It should come out clean, not greasy, and with no unpleasant smell. Imported boiling hams are generally cheaper than home-cured, but their flavour is not so delicate.

Cooked ham should be freshly sliced, the fat white, and the lean a delicate pink. Shoulder and collar make quite good substitutes for ham proper, especially if they are to be minced or cut up.

How to cook a ham. Ham must be soaked before cooking to remove the surplus salt. If a ham has been hung for a long time and is very dry it will need 24 hours soaking. Otherwise about 12 hours will be sufficient, especially if the water is changed once or twice.

Scrape and brush the ham to remove rust and trim off any coloured parts. (Remember that 'bloom' is the sign of a good ham.)

Poaching. Weigh the soaked joint and put it in a large pan, covered with cold water and without any seasoning. Bring it to the boil.

Meanwhile, heat together half a bottle of white wine, a small teaspoon of cloves, 8 peppercorns and sufficient water to cover the ham.

As soon as the first water boils throw it away and pour over the ham the liquid which you have prepared. Cover the pan and simmer for 25 minutes to the lb. When the ham is ready the skin will peel off easily.

Let the ham cool in the water in which it has cooked and when cold, drain it. Strip off the rind and trim away some of the fat.

Once poached, the ham can be glazed or braised, or covered with the traditional overcoat of breadcrumbs.

Glazing a ham. Put the ham on a baking dish and pour over it a glass of madeira, sherry or port. Cover it thickly with moist brown sugar and put it in a very hot oven (445° F, 230° C, Gas 8). After a quarter of an hour it will have a beautiful golden crust. Lower the heat to 355° F (180° C, Gas 4) and continue cooking for 15 minutes more.

Braising. Put the ham into a large, heavy casserole with half a bottle of madeira, sherry or white wine and cover it tightly. Cook in a very moderate oven (355° F, 180° C, Gas 4) for 45 minutes. Skim off the fat. This can be used to enrich the vegetables, such as peas, spinach, celery, or braised lettuce, with which the ham is served.

(Both glazing and braising can be carried out very successfully with tinned hams.)

Carving a ham. The classic carving of a ham is very complicated, and best learnt from an expert. It can, however, be treated in the same way as a leg of mutton (p. 109), provided you keep the slices very even and thin. According to a Victorian authority, a good carver should have been able to cover the whole of the then-popular Vauxhall Gardens with slices from one ham!

An American way of cooking a ham

Strip the rind from a ham which has been poached and allowed to cool in its own juice. Put it in a moderate oven (355° F, 180° C, Gas 4) with the fat side uppermost and bake it for 30 minutes.

Trim the fat to an even layer about ½-inch thick and score the surface in a pattern of criss-cross cuts about ¼-inch deep. If you wish, stick cloves at intervals into the diamond pattern.

Mix 5 tablespoons of Barbados sugar with a little water to form a paste which you spread over the surface of the ham. Put it back in the oven, raising the heat to 445° F, (230° C,

Gas 8) for 15 minutes, being careful that the glaze is covering the ham evenly.

Serve with a green vegetable, apple sauce or gooseberry jelly, and potato purée.

Instead of mixing water with the Barbados sugar try using honey, vinegar, crushed pineapple, or pineapple or orange juice. You can also replace the sugar mixture with orange marmalade, peach or apricot jam, or gooseberry jelly.

The ham looks very pretty if you decorate it with stars cut from orange or lemon peel, pinned on to the ham with cloves.

Gammon

The table on p. 153 shows how gammon, which is the hind leg of a pig cured together with the whole side of bacon, may be divided, and the characteristics and uses of the different cuts.

How to buy gammon. A whole joint of gammon is too large for an ordinary family but it costs much less per pound than buying the smaller joints separately. You can economize considerably by sharing a whole gammon with friends.

Good, lean rashers can be cut from the corner or middle gammon. These are usually about ¾-inch thick, while a gammon steak should be about 1-inch thick.

Cooking Gammon. A whole gammon should be soaked overnight and scraped in the same way as ham, then simmered with peppercorns and a couple of bay leaves. The cut end, before cooking, may be rubbed with brown sugar and the gammon should be allowed to remain for 2 hours in the water in which it is cooked before the skin is stripped off. If it is to be eaten cold, leave it on a board for 24 hours to set.

Gammon steaks are cut right across the leg and weigh about 1½ lb each. They should be soaked in cold water for an hour and then dried. The rind must be trimmed off and a series of snips cut into the border fat rather like a coarse fringe. The central bone should be removed and the steak will keep its shape better if you hold the edges of the hole left by the bone

GAMMON

Cuts	Characteristics	Cooking Suggestions
Gammon Slipper	The meat of all gammon cuts is delicate in flavour. The slipper is a small, lean, family cut weighing about $1\frac{1}{2}$ lb.	Gammon is used for traditional English boiled bacon. Slipper may be boiled whole, or be cut into rashers.
Corner Gammon	Lean and well-flavoured cut which weighs about 4 lb.	Excellent boiled in the piece and served either hot or cold. Can also be grilled in thick rashers.
Middle Gammon	Succulent cut with plenty of lean. Weight, about 5 lb.	Boil and serve hot or cold; or cut into thick rashers and fry or grill.
Gammon Hock	Weighs about $4\frac{1}{2}$ lb.	This joint is best baked after being par-boiled. It is equally good hot or cold.

together with two small skewers placed crosswise. Before grilling a gammon steak brush it over with butter.

Gammon rashers can be fried or grilled after having the rind removed and a series of snips cut into the fat round the edge. Brush the rasher with melted butter or fat before grilling.

The following ham recipes will be more economical if they are made with shoulder or collar.

Ham, Celeriac and Poached Egg Canapes Economical

½ celeriac root ✦ salt ¼ lemon	Peel the celeriac and cut it in four thick slices. Put it in boiling salted water with the lemon and cook until tender.
2 tablespoons butter ✦ 2 teaspoons cornflour or arrowroot ✦ meat extract	Warm the butter and flour together and stir in, slowly, the meat extract and a glass of the liquid in which the celeriac was cooked. Cook gently for 10 minutes. The sauce should be light and translucent.
3 tablespoons butter ✦ 4 slices bread	Cut 4 round croûtons and fry them golden-brown in hot butter. Keep them warm on a dish.
2 fairly thick slices ham	Cut each slice of ham in two and let them colour in the frying pan. Lay ham and a celeriac slice on each croûton.
4 eggs	Poach the eggs in water with a dash of vinegar.
1 tablespoon madeira, marsala or sherry (optional) ✦ 1 teaspoon chopped parsley	Drain and place one, bathed in sauce, on each croûton. (A tablespoonful of madeira, marsala or sherry improves the sauce.) Sprinkle with parsley and serve.

If you do not wish to use celeriac, replace it by a cupful of spinach purée. In this case, substitute a glass of bouillon for the meat extract and the water.

Ham and Cauliflower Cheese Very economical

1 cup white breadcrumbs	Stir the milk and breadcrumbs over a

1 glass milk ✦ 2 tablespoons butter ✦ salt and pepper ✦ a pinch nutmeg

gentle fire until the sauce is thick, then add the butter. Season.

4 slices ham ✦ a small cauliflower

Chop the ham coarsely. Cook the cauliflower in boiling salted water. Drain and chop it. Fill a buttered fireproof dish with alternate layers of cauliflower, ham and bread sauce, finishing with a layer of cauliflower.

2 hard-boiled eggs ✦ 1 teaspoon minced parsley 3 tablespoons brown breadcrumbs ✦ 4 tablespoons butter ✦ 2 tablespoons grated parmesan

Chop the eggs finely and sprinkle the cauliflower with egg, parsley, breadcrumbs and melted butter. Top with grated cheese and brown for 20 minutes in a hot oven (425° F, 220° C, Gas 7).

You can make this dish with remains of cold meat instead of ham.

Ham and Leeks au Gratin Very economical

This is a family dish which can be made with leeks or spinach—or chicory if you are feeling more extravagant.

8 leeks *or* 1 lb spinach *or* 8 heads of chicory

Cook the whole vegetables in boiling salted water and drain.

4 hard-boiled eggs ✦ 4 slices ham

Cut the eggs in half lengthwise. Divide the vegetables in 4 and wrap each portion in a slice of ham. Arrange them in a buttered fireproof dish surrounded by eggs.

3 tablespoons flour ✦ 3 tablespoons butter ✦ 2 glasses milk ✦ salt and pepper ✦ 5 tablespoons grated cheese

Work the butter and flour together and stir in the milk over a low fire. Season, and cook for 15 minutes. Add the cheese, mixing well and being careful that the sauce does not boil. Pour it over the ham and eggs and brown in the oven or under the grill.

Ham Soufflé Very economical

You can also make this soufflé with the remains of cooked chicken. A small tin of button mushrooms, very finely chopped and added at the same time as the meat, makes a pleasant variation with either ham or chicken.

3 tablespoons butter ✦ 2 tablespoons flour ✦ 1½ glasses milk ✦ 3 tablespoons each grated parmesan and gruyère cheese	Make a sauce with butter, flour and milk and cook for 10 minutes on a slow fire. Stir in the cheese, and pepper generously.
4 slices ham ✦ 3 or 4 eggs	Chop the ham finely. Remove the pan from the fire and whisk in the ham and the egg yolks. Beat the whites stiffly, fold them in, and pour the mixture into a buttered soufflé dish. Cook at 380° F (195° C, Gas 5) for 35 minutes without opening the oven door.

BACON

Bacon has been a popular food in England for at least 700 years, and is mentioned by Chaucer. Some people claim that the word is French in origin while others maintain that bacon comes from a German word *Backen*, meaning wild sows. In the past the French used '*bacon*' to mean pork in general and especially the back-fat.

There are many different ways of producing bacon. In this country mild-cured is the most popular and the following is a method in general use:

Whole sides of bacon are cured by being injected with brine and then steeped in large brine tanks for four days or so. Under careful control the brine matures like wine and is added to and used again and again. After steeping, the meat is stacked in a maturing chamber from seven to eleven days. At this stage the bacon is 'green'.

Bacon can be smoked in a variety of ways, but a common industrial method is to hang the salted sides, dusted with very fine pea meal, in a specially ventilated chamber over smouldering oak or deal saw-dust for from 36 to 60 hours. This is usually called a Wiltshire cure.

The popularity of mild-cured bacon is fairly recent. In the

past it was hard-cured by a dry process and often required soaking before being cooked. This was troublesome but, on the other hand, the bacon kept better and, unlike present-day bacon, actually improved with keeping.

Bacon should be stored in a cool place where it will keep for about 10–12 days in winter but only about 4–5 days in summer. Bacon must not be put in a deep-freeze and if stored in a domestic refrigerator should be well wrapped.

Buying bacon. The lean of bacon should be an appetizing pink, moist but not wet. (Bacon which is too damp will not keep well.) The fat should be white with no yellow patches or greenish tinge.

If possible, have your rashers cut to the thickness you require for a particular purpose. In the old days this was taken as a matter of course but now it is rare to find an assistant who will, with a good grace, slice bacon to a particular setting.

Since bacon loses some weight during smoking, 'green' bacon should be cheaper than smoked. One firm produces a sweet-cured bacon to their own recipe. This is sold packaged and with the rinds removed, which is a great time-saver. This bacon is cut at machine setting No. 6.

The table on p. 158 will give you an idea of the various cuts of bacon and what you can do with them. Fore and gammon cuts are usually less expensive in the winter, while middle cuts should be cheaper in the summer months.

To prepare bacon. Remove any bone from the rashers and cut off the rinds singly or several at a time using, for speed, kitchen scissors. Each rasher should be flattened with a heavy knife so that it spreads, and fries more rapidly.

How to fry bacon. Heat the pan and lay the bacon in it with the lean part of each rasher overlapping the fat of the one next door. Fry the rashers gently, turning them once. When the fat is clear the bacon is ready to eat, but some people like it crisp and cook it a little longer. Take care, though, that it does not become dry and brittle.

BACON

Fore Cuts	Characteristics	Cooking Suggestions
Fore hock including butt, small hock, fore slipper.	Economical cut. Weight, about 8 lb. Can be bought whole, boned and rolled, or divided.	Suitable for boiling.
Prime Collar	Inexpensive cut weighing about 6 lb.	Excellent boiled whole. Rashers can be fried or grilled.
End of Collar	Small, inexpensive cut weighing about 2 lb.	Good for boiling or braising. Should be skinned and lightly pressed after cooking.
Middle Cuts		
Top Streaky	Makes economical rashers or can be boned and rolled whole. Weighs about $1\frac{1}{4}$ lb.	Boil if left whole. Rashers may be grilled or fried.
Prime Streaky	The best streaky cut with an excellent flavour. Weight, about $5\frac{1}{2}$ lb.	Boil in one piece, or cook as rashers.
Thin Streaky	Economical cut for grilling or frying. Weighs about $1\frac{1}{2}$ lb. All streaky should be thinly sliced. (No. 4–5.)	Fried or grilled rashers are particularly good when well crisped.
Top Back	A good lean cut. Weight, about $2\frac{1}{4}$ lb.	Can be boiled or braised whole, or cut into thin rashers and grilled.

BACON (continued)

Middle Cuts	Characteristics	Cooking Suggestions
Short Back	One of the best breakfast cuts. Weighs about 5 lb. Should be cut at No. 6 or 7.	Fry or grill in rashers.
Back and Ribs	Similar to short back but less fat. Weight, about 6¾ lb. Rashers should be cut rather thicker than streaky ones.	Makes good rashers for grilling and frying.
Long Back	The choicest lean cut. It is wider than short back and should be sliced thinly. Weight, about 2½ lb.	Grill rapidly or fry gently.
Flank	Economical cut for boiling or frying. Weighs about 2¾ lb.	Useful in recipes where chopped bacon is required. Good with liver.
Oyster	Excellent small joint. Similar to short back. Weight, about 1½ lb.	Rashers, which are rather fat, are excellent with liver or for tying over the breasts of poultry.

Grilled bacon. Pre-heat the grill and arrange the rashers with the fat overlapping the lean. Turn when they are just beginning to brown, and grill the other side.

Oven-cooked bacon. Heating the oven especially to cook bacon is obviously wasteful, but if you are using it for something else, or are lucky enough to have an AGA or similar stove, try cooking your bacon in a greased fireproof dish. Lay the fat of each rasher over the lean of the next and cook it for about 10 minutes at 380° F (195° C, Gas 5).

Toasted bacon. Bacon is delicious toasted over an open fire, especially if this is of wood. As children we used to love cooking bacon over the nursery fire but nowadays there are few nannies willing to clear up the mess—and not so many nursery fires either.

OFFAL—OX

Name	Characteristics	Cooking Suggestions
Liver	Inexpensive. Rather coarse in flavour and texture.	Should be soaked before using (1 hour in cold salt water). Best braised, or sliced and served with a good sauce.
Kidney	Cheaper than other forms of kidney. Has rather a strong flavour. Weighs about 1½ lb.	Generally used for steak and kidney pudding. Can be braised or made into soup.
Brains	Inexpensive. Weight, from 1–1½ lb.	May be blanched and then sautéd, fried or used to make a sauce.
Sweetbreads	Fairly expensive. In the older animals the more delicate thymus gland has already atrophied and only the long pancreas gland remains.	Cook in the same way as brains.
Tongue	Fairly expensive, but there is no waste if the tongue is short-cut to remove gristle, etc. Sold either fresh, salted or smoked. Weight from 4–6 lb.	Can be boiled and eaten hot or cold, stewed, fried or braised.
Tripe	Very cheap. Is usually sold cleaned and blanched, but requires further cooking.	Is excellent crisp-fried with onions or sliced finely and simmered in a spicy sauce. Normally served in England as a greyish stew.
Tail	Fairly cheap and excellently flavoured.	Makes a good stew or soup.

OFFAL—OX (continued)

Name	Characteristics	Cooking Suggestions
Heart	Has a good flavour but is somewhat tough and indigestible. Weight, 3–4 lb.	Requires long soaking in cold, salt water. Is best braised, after stuffing with a savoury mixture to which herbs and extra fat have been added.
Ox cheek and head trimmings	Very cheap and generally used for manufacturing of animal food.	Can be stewed or made into brawn.

OFFAL—CALF

Name	Characteristics	Cooking Suggestions
Liver	Usually the most expensive kind of liver, tender and very delicate in flavour.	May be roasted or braised whole, or sliced and fried or sautéd.
Kidneys	Larger than lamb's kidneys but more delicate in flavour.	Excellent roast, braised, grilled or prepared in a sauce.
Brains	Reasonable in cost. Weight, about ½ lb.	After blanching, can be sautéd, served in sauce or used in a soufflé.
Sweetbreads	Very delicate and expensive. A pair serves two people.	After blanching may be braised, grilled, sautéd, or used for *timbales*, escalopes or garnishes.
Tongue	Of fine flavour and texture and not too expensive. Usually sold fresh, but may be salted. Weight, 1–2 lb.	Poach and serve with sauce, or eat cold.

OFFAL—CALF (continued)

Name	Characteristics	Cooking Suggestions
Heart	Reasonable in price and of quite good flavour. Like all heart meat, is lean and inclined to be dry.	Stuff and roast, or slice and sauté. Must be well basted and is improved by a sharp sauce.
Head	The meat is rich and gelatinous and easily digested. Heads are generally sold boned and blanched. They make a variety of economical dishes.	Usually boiled and served with a variety of sauces. Forms the basis of a mock turtle soup.
Feet	Inexpensive.	Used to enrich the consistency of many dishes such as *bœuf à la mode*. Makes excellent meat jelly.

OFFAL—SHEEP AND LAMB

Name	Characteristics	Cooking Suggestions
Liver	Cheaper than calf's liver and not so good.	May be cooked in the same way as calf's liver or used in pâtés, etc. It is much improved by a piquant sauce.
Kidneys	Lamb's kidneys are tender and delicate in flavour. They are often left attached to the meat, whilst sheep's kidneys are usually sold separately. Both are reasonable in price.	Grilled, fry, sauté, or serve on toast or devilled.

OFFAL—SHEEP AND LAMB (continued)

Name	Characteristics	Cooking Suggestions
Brains	Inexpensive. Considered inferior to calf's brains. Weight, from 4–6 oz.	After blanching, may be stewed, served on toast, or made into a pudding with tongue.
Sweetbreads	Smaller than calf's sweetbreads and usually sold by weight. Fairly expensive and very delicate.	Prepare like calf's sweetbreads. Excellent for ragoûts.
Tongue	Weight, about 8–12 oz each. Not expensive. Are sometimes sold partially cooked.	Can be braised, boiled, fried, or prepared in a sauce.
Heart	Very good value if carefully cooked. One sheep's heart will serve two people, but one lamb's heart makes a single portion.	Usually stuffed and roasted; should be basted frequently. May be sliced and sautéd.
Head	Extremely cheap.	Boil and serve with brain sauce or, after boiling, prepare au gratin in the oven.
Feet (or Trotters)	Cheap and tasty. Sold blanched and partially cooked.	May be stewed, or baked with tomatoes, etc.
Paunch and Pluck	Usually sold for haggis. The pluck consists of the heart, liver and lungs (or lites).	The paunch is used as a container for the haggis and the pluck is incorporated in the filling.
Lamb's fry (or Test Glands)	These are from young ram lambs. They are inexpensive, but few butchers stock them.	Excellent sliced and sautéd in butter, or used in timbales, fricassees or garnishes.

OFFAL—PIG

Name	Characteristics	Cooking Suggestions
Liver	Less expensive and not so delicate as that of calf or lamb.	Can be grilled or used in stews.
Kidneys	Larger than sheep's kidneys and stronger in flavour. Also cheaper.	Soak and blanch pig's kidneys before cooking. If grilled, because of their size, they should be cut in half lengthwise. They can be used for sautés and ragoûts.
Pig's Fry (Heart, lites (lungs), liver and sweetbreads)	Most economical buy, but not always easy to find. Lites are now usually fed to animals. Pig's fry is sometimes called haslet or harslet.	Very good baked with vegetables and herbs, or sliced and fried.

NOTE: Pig's head, including the brains and tongue, is sold attached to the carcase, and is not classed as offal.

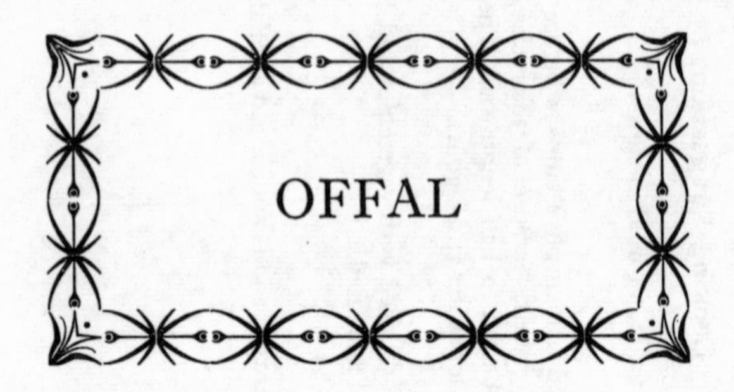

OFFAL

Many people appreciate the wonderful variety of economical dishes which can be made from offal. Others, unfortunately, regard it as something for which they competed fiercely during the war but which is now best pushed to the back of the mind along with whale and snook.

Most forms of offal are very nourishing and none, except perhaps calf's liver and kidneys, are dear compared with a corresponding cut of meat.

Offal must be eaten fresh. It will keep in the refrigerator for a day and should be loosely bunched in foil so that air can get in. Greaseproof paper is unsatisfactory as it sticks to the moist surfaces.

The tables on pages 162–6 describe the various forms of offal usually on sale in butcher's shops.

Liver

Of all forms of offal, liver has the most tonic and nourishing qualities. Rich in iron, copper and vitamins, it is also used in the preparation of certain medicines.

The nutritive value of the various kinds of liver is more or less the same, but their culinary value and price differ considerably.

Buying liver. Liver should be smooth and glossy without any bluish tint. Very dark liver usually comes from an older animal.

You can buy liver in a piece or ask the butcher to slice it for you, but don't expect the average butcher to slice it thinly unless you insist. Allow about 4 oz for each person.

Calf's liver is the most expensive and the most delicate. Choose the palest and see that it is sliced evenly.

Lamb's and pig's liver are both quite tender and well-flavoured though sheep's liver is coarser.

Ox liver is coarse in flavour and texture. It is worth soaking the sliced liver in salted water for a couple of hours before using, and then blanching it before cooking.

Preparation. Liver should be wiped with a damp cloth and all the veins and outside skin removed.

Calf's and lamb's liver only need very little cooking. They are excellent dipped in seasoned flour and sautéd in hot butter or oil. They can also be grilled after being well brushed with oil or melted butter. The crust which forms on the outside adds greatly to the flavour. Only turn the liver once, when the juice gathers in beads on the surface (after 3–4 minutes in a frying pan or 4–5 minutes under the grill).

Because of their delicate flavour calf's and lamb's liver should be cooked as simply as possible. Ox, pig's and sheep's liver, which have a much stronger taste, must be well done but kept moist. They are really best braised. Pig's liver is useful as an addition to pâtés.

Brochettes of Liver Moderately expensive

1 lb calf's or lamb's liver ½ lb bacon	Cut the liver in 1-inch squares and season. Thread the bacon, cut in squares of the same size, on 4 skewers, alternately with liver, pushing the pieces well together.
2 tablespoons oil	Sprinkle with oil and grill gently for 6–10 minutes, turning once.

This dish can be made with kidneys instead of liver.

Variation:

1 egg ✦ 1 teaspoon water 3 tablespoons breadcrumbs 3 tablespoons butter	Roll the skewered liver and bacon in egg beaten with water, and then in breadcrumbs. Heat the butter to smoking point and fry the brochettes for 10 minutes, turning frequently. Put them on a dish to keep hot.
juice of ½ lemon ✦ chopped parsley	Stir the lemon juice into the caramel in the pan, scraping the bottom well. Pour the sauce over the brochettes and dust them with parsley.

Roast Liver Moderately expensive

Buy the liver in one piece. Remove the skin and veins, and let it soak in milk for half a day. Drain and dry it.

1 lb liver ✦ 4 oz 'green' streaky bacon	Cut the bacon into thin strips and lard the liver (p. 35).
4 oz smoked bacon ✦ 2 onions ✦ 5 mushrooms a stalk celery ✦ 1 teaspoon grated lemon peel	Chop all the ingredients very finely and line with them the bottom of a buttered fireproof dish, laying the liver on top.
salt and pepper ✦ 4 tablespoons butter ✦ 4 tablespoons cream	Season and sprinkle the liver with melted butter and cream. Cook in a moderate oven (355° F, 180° C, Gas 4) for 15 minutes.
1 teaspoon flour ✦ ½ glass bouillon	Mix the flour with warm bouillon and pour it round the meat. Continue to cook, basting every 10 minutes (½ hour for calf's liver and 40 minutes for ox or pig's liver).
juice of ½ lemon	Work the sauce gently through a sieve. Season it and add the lemon juice.

Terrine of Minced Liver Economical

1 lb liver ✦ 2 tablespoons fat	Chop the liver coarsely. Cook it in hot fat for a few minutes and put it into a lidded fireproof dish.
2 stalks celery ✦ 2 onions 2 tomatoes	Chop the celery and onions and let them soften in the frying pan, adding more fat if necessary. Remove skin and pips from the tomatoes and chop them.

1½ cups uncooked rice
salt and pepper
2½ glasses bouillon ✦ 3 tablespoons tomato purée

Mix the rice with the vegetables and liver in the fireproof dish and season. Dilute the tomato purée in hot bouillon and pour it into the rice and liver mixture. Cover the dish and cook in an oven pre-heated to 355° F (180° C, Gas 4) for ½ hour or until the liquid is completely absorbed and the rice is soft.

Liver with Herbs Moderately expensive

This dish may be made with kidney instead of liver.

4 tablespoons butter ✦ 2 fillets anchovy ✦ 2 tablespoons of chopped parsley, chives and chervil

Mash the anchovies with a fork until they form a smooth paste. Melt the butter and cook the herbs and anchovies for 3 minutes over a low fire.

4 slices liver ✦ salt and pepper ✦ 1 tablespoon flour

Cut each slice of liver in two. Season, dip in flour and cook, very gently, in the same pan for 5–10 minutes, turning once. Raise the heat towards the end to brown the liver.

juice of ½ lemon ✦ 1 teaspoon Worcestershire sauce

Add the lemon juice and Worcestershire sauce and heat for a moment before serving.

The anchovies will disappear completely in the sauce, leaving only an elusive flavour.

Liver or Kidney Pilaff Moderately expensive

4 tablespoons butter ✦ 1 cup rice ✦ 3½ cups boiling water ✦ 1 large cube chicken broth concentrate

Heat the butter in a flameproof casserole, add the rice and let it colour slightly. Dilute the chicken cube in boiling water and pour it on to the rice. Close the lid tightly and cook until the liquid is completely absorbed. (The time will depend on the type of rice and you may need slightly more or less liquid.)

1 lb liver or kidney ✦ 2 tablespoons butter or oil
1 tablespoon flour

Cut the liver or kidney in fairly fine slices and roll them in flour. Brown in oil or butter, shaking the pan. Put the

	rice on a hot dish, topped with liver or kidney.
1 glass bouillon *or* ½ glass madeira and ½ glass bouillon	Deglaze the pan with bouillon plain, or mixed with madeira. Boil for a moment and pour the liquid over the rice.

Chinese Pig's Liver Very economical

Chinese methods require long and careful preparation for a very short period of cooking.

It is essential to have everything ready and within easy reach, and from the moment when the pan is on the fire to continue shaking it backwards and forwards with a gentle, regular movement. Choose a large frying pan.

14 oz pig's liver ✦ 2 slices ham	Cut the liver in long, thin strips. Chop the ham coarsely.
a small cauliflower ✦ 2 tablespoons dried mushrooms	Open up the cauliflower and use only the flowerets. Soak the mushrooms in tepid water for 1 hour. Drain, and dry them on kitchen paper. Cut them in pieces.
2 tablespoons lard	Heat the lard to smoking point in a large heavy frying pan.
1 tablespoon garden peas (fresh if possible) ✦ 1 tablespoon soya sauce ✦ salt	Toss the cauliflower, ham and peas in the frying pan until they are just golden brown, add soya sauce and salt and then the liver and mushrooms.
4 tablespoons bouillon	Pour in the bouillon and cook for a few minutes more over a lively heat, shaking the pan all the time.

Liver Balls Economical

For this dish ox or pig's liver are suitable.

2 tablespoons lard ✦ 1 tablespoon fresh peas salt ✦ 1 tablespoon soya sauce	Heat the lard in a large frying pan. Throw in the cauliflower, peas and ham and let them brown. Add salt and soya sauce, then the liver and mushrooms.

4 tablespoons bouillon	Moisten with bouillon and continue to cook over lively heat for a few minutes, shaking the pan all the time.
1 lb liver ✦ 4 oz 'green' bacon ✦ 3 slices bread 3 tablespoons white wine 1 teaspoon minced parsley ✦ 2 egg yolks ✦ 1 tablespoon grated parmesan cheese (optional)	Soak the bread in wine, squeeze it dry and crumble it finely. Chop the liver and bacon and mix all together to form 8 balls.
a piece caul fat	Dip the caul fat in hot water. Spread it out and cut into 8 pieces. Wrap up each liver ball.
1 egg ✦ 1 teaspoon water 1 teaspoon oil ✦ breadcrumbs ✦ 4 tablespoons butter	Dip the balls first in egg beaten with water and oil, then in breadcrumbs. Brown them in butter, lower the heat and cook, slowly, for 10 minutes more.
2 tablespoons butter ✦ 1 teaspoon each chopped parsley and chives ✦ 1 tablespoon lemon juice	Stir in the butter, herbs and lemon juice and serve the balls with their own sauce.

Kidneys

Calf's kidneys are the most expensive. Those of lamb, whilst not so dear, are still very delicate in flavour. The food value of all kidneys is much the same.

Buying kidneys. The surface of ox and calf's kidney is divided into sections and can easily be distinguished from those of sheep or pigs, which are smooth and haricot-bean-shaped. All kidneys are enveloped in fat which is often stripped off before they are sold. This fat is excellent rendered down and used for frying and roasting.

Allow about 4–5 oz of ox or calf's kidney for each person; one pig's or sheep's kidney, or two of lamb.

Kidneys, if they are to have a good flavour, must be eaten quickly and should not be kept longer than 24 hours in the refrigerator.

Preparation. Lamb's kidneys are usually grilled and should be slightly underdone so that they are a delicate pink inside.

Calf's kidneys generally are used for sautés, or cooked in a sauce.

When grilling kidneys, split them lengthwise without separating the halves, and keep them flat by means of two small skewers arranged crosswise and stuck into the edges of the kidney, Grill the cut side first.

Calf's kidneys should not be cooked too long nor 'seized' over too hot a fire or they will become tough and very strong in flavour.

Ox, sheep's and pig's kidneys have a rather pronounced taste. Before cooking them you should:

Skin them, and cut them up if necessary.
Remove the core (nail scissors are ideal for this operation).
Put them into a colander and drench them several times in boiling water.
Sauté them in hot fat.
Put them back into the colander and let them drain for 10 minutes. Throw away the fat and dark juice which has run out.

Ox kidney is generally used in this country for pies and puddings, though it is good stewed, or served in a sauce.

If stewed or casseroled in the oven, kidneys are often left whole with part of the fat surrounding them. This greatly improves their texture and flavour.

All kinds of kidneys are much improved by being flambé (p. 35).

Grilled Kidneys Moderately expensive

Ox kidneys are not suitable for this dish.

1¼ lb kidney ✦ 8 thin rashers bacon	If possible, leave a little fat on the split kidneys. Keep them flat with small skewers. Cover the cut sides with bacon.
salt and pepper ✦ 4 table-spoons melted butter	Season the kidneys and drench them with butter. Grill gently 5–6 minutes each side, a good 2 inches from the heat.

Serve with grilled mushrooms and tomatoes, watercress and maître d'hôtel butter (p. 201).

Kidneys with Mushrooms Economical

Use ox or pig's kidneys for this dish.

1¼ lb kidney ✦ 1 tablespoon fat	Prepare the kidneys as above, chopping them coarsely.
2 tablespoons butter ✦ 8 mushrooms ✦ 3 shallots 1 tablespoon flour ✦ ½ glass red or white wine ½ glass bouillon ✦ salt and pepper	Heat the butter in a flameproof casserole and brown the sliced mushrooms. Add the minced shallots, sprinkle with flour, stir in wine and warm bouillon, season and simmer for 15 minutes.
2 tablespoons cream ✦ 1 tablespoon minced parsley	Return the kidneys to the sauce, then add the cream. Heat gently without boiling. Sprinkle with parsley and serve.

Kidneys with Mushrooms Expensive

1¼ lb calf's or sheep's kidney ✦ 1 tablespoon butter	Slice the kidneys thinly, brown them in butter and drain them in a colander keeping the juice.
4 or 5 mushrooms	Brown the sliced mushrooms in the same butter and add them to the kidneys. Season.
1 tablespoon flour ✦ ½ glass white wine ✦ ½ glass bouillon	Sprinkle the pan with flour, add the wine and warm bouillon, stirring to avoid lumps. Cook gently for 10 minutes. The sauce must be thick. Add the juice from the kidneys.
4 sheep's kidneys ✦ 4 large round slices white bread 3 tablespoons butter	Cut the kidneys in half and remove the cores. Fry the croûtons in hot butter and set them aside to keep hot.
2 tablespoon butter ✦ salt and pepper	Add more butter to the pan. Brown the kidneys on both sides, season and keep them hot, one on each croûton.
½ teaspoon cornflour or arrowroot ✦ ½ glass good red wine ✦ salt and pepper 1 teaspoon butter ✦ 1 teaspoon minced parsley	Put the cornflour, mixed with a little water, into the frying pan and stir in the wine. Mix well, season and cook for 5 minutes. At the last moment, add in the butter, pour the sauce over the kidneys and sprinkle with parsley.

Kidneys with Onions Economical

4 onions ✦ 6 shallots ✦ 2 tablespoons butter ✦ ½ glass bouillon or white wine	Heat the butter in a small saucepan and brown the onions and shallots, cut in pieces. Season, moisten with bouillon and cook for 20 minutes. Put the vegetables through a sieve or blender.
1¼ lb ox or pig's kidney 2 tablespoons butter ✦ salt and pepper ✦ 1 tablespoon lemon juice ✦ 1 teaspoon minced parsley	Slice the kidneys thinly and brown them rapidly in a frying pan. Season, add the onion purée and, after heating a moment or two, the lemon juice. Sprinkle with parsley and serve with small croûtons of fried bread.

Kidneys on Croûtons with Red Wine Economical

4 sheep's kidneys	Cut the kidneys in two lengthwise and remove the cores.
8 slices white bread ✦ 3 tablespoons butter	Trim the bread into rounds and brown them in butter in a large frying pan. Put them on a dish.
2 tablespoons butter ✦ salt and pepper	Add more butter to the pan. Brown the kidneys on both sides and season. Put each half kidney on a croûton and keep hot.
½ teaspoon cornflour ✦ ½ glass good red wine ✦ salt and pepper ✦ 1 teaspoon butter	Mix the cornflour with a little cold water and put it in the frying pan together with the wine. Stir well and cook for 5 minutes. Season if necessary, add the butter, and pour the sauce over the kidneys.
1 teaspoon chopped parsley	Dust with parsley and serve.

Accompany the kidneys with button mushrooms and small onions sautéd in butter.

Brochettes of Kidneys and Mushrooms Moderately expensive

8–10 large mushrooms 1 tablespoon butter	Wash, dry and slice the mushrooms in half lengthwise. Soften them in butter and let them cool.

1¼ lb kidney ✦ 4 oz 'green' bacon ✦ 2 tablespoons melted butter ✦ 1 slice stale white bread	Cut the kidney in even-sized pieces and the bacon to match. Thread mushrooms, kidney and bacon alternately on metal skewers and sprinkle with melted butter. Roll them in white breadcrumbs.
2 tablespoons butter	Heat the butter in a frying pan and cook the brochettes for 15 minutes, turning them frequently.
2 tablespoons butter teaspoon chopped parsley tablespoon lemon juice	Work the butter together with the parsley and lemon juice and put a pat on each brochette just before serving.

Rognons de Veau à la Liégeoise Expensive

2 tablespoons butter ✦ 2 calf's kidneys ✦ salt and pepper	Leave the kidneys whole. Season, and sizzle them lightly in butter. Close the lid of the pan and simmer for 20 minutes.
4 or 5 juniper berries ✦ 3 tablespoons gin	Crush the berries and put them, with the gin, into a small saucepan. Warm for a moment and then pour the flaming alcohol over the kidneys. Set them aside on a hot dish.
2 tablespoons bouillon	Deglaze the pan with hot bouillon. Pour the sauce over the kidneys and serve.

Calf's Kidneys with Mustard Expensive

For this recipe buy, if possible, kidneys with the fat still attached.

2 kidneys ✦ 2 tablespoons butter	Season the kidneys and leave them whole. Melt the butter in a flameproof casserole, brown the kidneys lightly and cook with the lid on for 20 minutes (preferably in the oven).
8 mushrooms ✦ 2 tablespoons butter	Slice the mushrooms finely and brown them in a frying pan. Add them to the kidney and cook for another 10 minutes.
2 tablespoons light French mustard ✦ 3 tablespoons thick cream	Stir the cream and mustard into the sauce round the kidneys, making sure it does not boil. As soon as the sauce is well mixed, serve.

Sweetbreads

Though 'throat' and 'heart' breads are priced and treated differently they both come from the same gland, the thymus. As an animal gets older this gland becomes smaller. Only in oxen does a usable part of the 'heart' bread remain. The rounded 'heart' breads are very delicate; the 'throat' bread, which is longer and more untidy in appearance, is generally mixed with other ingredients in a timbale, or used as a garnish.

The pancreas or stomach bread is sometimes referred to as a sweetbread. It has a different, though quite pleasant flavour.

Allow 4–5 oz for each portion.

Preparation. To keep sweetbreads as white as possible soak them for at least 4 hours in cold water which should be changed several times. Then put them into cold salted water, and bring them slowly to the boil. As soon as the water is boiling lift them out.

Holding the sweetbreads under a trickle of cold water and using the point of a knife, remove the black veins and the skin which covers them. Wrap them in a cloth and put them to cool between two plates, or on a board beneath a plate with a weight on top to flatten them.

The sweetbreads can then be larded (p. 35) with strips of fat bacon, tongue, ham or truffles; cut into escalopes about ½-inch thick, or cooked just as they are.

One of the best ways of cooking sweetbreads is to sauté them, egg-and-breadcrumbed, in butter. Deglaze (p. 35) the pan in which they have cooked with bouillon, white wine, lemon juice or madeira. Serve them with boiled potatoes and vegetables such as sorrel, spinach, green peas or braised lettuce.

Braised Sweetbreads Expensive

1¼ lb blanched and pressed sweetbreads 4 oz 'green' bacon	Lard the sweetbreads with fine strips of bacon and dice the remainder of the bacon.
2 carrots ✦ 2 stalks celery 1 onion ✦ 1 tablespoon fat salt and pepper	Chop the vegetables finely, brown them with the bacon and season. Lay the sweetbreads on a bed of vegetables in a deep fireproof dish.

1 glass bouillon	Moisten with bouillon, cover and cook in a moderate oven (380° F, 195° C, Gas 5) for ½ hour, basting occasionally. Remove the lid, increase the heat, and brown the sweetbreads for 10 minutes. Put them on a dish to keep hot.
1 tablespoon butter ½ teaspoon cornflour	Strain the liquid, and add it, little by little, to the butter and flour which you have worked together in a small saucepan. When the sauce has thickened, pour it over the sweetbreads.

Beignets de Ris de veau Expensive

To make the batter, which must stand for two hours:

½ cup flour ✦ 1 tablespoon oil ✦ salt ✦ 4 tablespoons water ✦ 1 egg white	Put the flour in a bowl, make a hollow in the middle and pour in first the water and then the oil, stirring all the time with a wooden spoon until the paste is smooth. Beat the white of egg and fold it into the batter just before using.
1¼ lb sweetbreads (or brains)	Put the blanched sweetbreads into cold veal stock or bouillon and poach very gently for 40 minutes. Drain the sweetbreads, cut them in large pieces and put them into a soup plate.
2 tablespoons oil ✦ juice of ½ lemon ✦ salt and pepper	Season the sweetbreads and let them marinate in oil and lemon at least ½ hour. Dip them in batter and deep-fry until they are golden brown. Drain and serve.

Accompany the sweetbreads with fried parsley (p. 68), steamed potatoes and, if you like, tomato sauce (p. 203).

Sweetbread Filling for Vol-au-Vent

Moderately expensive

Unless you are an expert at flaky pastry, it will probably be more satisfactory to buy the vol-au-vent or bouchée cases ready-made.

3 tablespoons butter ✦ 3 tablespoons flour ✦ 2½ cups veal stock or chicken bouillon ✦ 8 mushrooms	Melt the butter, work in the flour and add the hot bouillon, carefully avoiding lumps. Cook gently for 15 minutes. Add the finely sliced mushrooms and cook another 5 minutes.
1 lb 'throat' breads, blanched ✦ 2 slices ham	Poach the sweetbreads for 40 minutes, drain and cool and cut them, like the ham, in small pieces. Add both to the sauce.
2 egg yolks ✦ salt and pepper ✦ 1 teaspoon minced parsley ✦ chicken stock	Put the egg yolks in a bowl and whisk in some hot stock. When the yolks have thickened stir them into the sweetbread mixture, watching that they do not boil. Adjust the seasoning and fill the pastry cases.

If you are cooking for a very special occasion, add some pieces of truffle and cock's combs.

Brains and Amourettes

Brains are very nourishing and rich in phosphorus but they do not suit everyone. Calf's brains are considered the most delicate.

You should allow about 4–5 oz of brains for each person and the following table shows roughly how this works out:

	Approximate Weight	*Usual Number of Servings*
Ox brains	1– 1½ lb	4–5
Calf's brains	9–10 oz	2
Sheep's brains	5 oz	1
Lamb's brains	3½ oz	1
Pig's brains	5 oz	1

The spinal marrow of calves is very delicate in flavour and used a great deal in France, under the name *amourettes*, for filling vol-au-vent cases and so on. That of oxen is not quite so good. *Amourettes* should be prepared and blanched in the same way as brains.

Preparation. Soak brains (or *amourettes*) for 15 minutes in cold water to which you have added a little vinegar. Strip off the membrane and remove any blood clots. This can be done more easily under a running tap. Once they are cleaned, the brains should be left to soak in cold water, which is changed from time to time, for at least an hour.

Prepare a court-bouillon by putting a sliced medium-sized onion, a piece of carrot and a stalk of celery, a teaspoonful of vinegar, salt, pepper and a bouquet garni (p. 35) into a small saucepan with enough cold water to cover the brains, and bringing them to the boil.

Plunge the brains into the boiling liquid, lower the heat so that the surface just quivers, and poach for 10–15 minutes. Drain the brains (or *amourettes*) and prepare them according to the recipe you have chosen.

Fried Brains Moderately expensive

1 lb brains ✦ 2 tablespoons olive oil ✦ juice of ½ lemon salt and pepper
1 egg ✦ 1 teaspoon water 1 teaspoon oil ✦ breadcrumbs
½ cup olive oil or 5 tablespoons butter

Cut the blanched and poached brains in thick slices. Marinate them for ½ hour in seasoned oil and lemon juice. Beat the egg, oil and water and coat the brains. Dip the pieces in breadcrumbs and let them rest for 10 minutes. Make the fat smoking hot and brown the brains for 4 minutes on each side. Serve them with fried parsley (p. 68).

Decorate each slice of brains with a rolled anchovy.

Brains with Black Butter Economical

1 lb brains, blanched and poached ✦ 5 tablespoons butter
1 tablespoon vinegar ✦ 1 tablespoon capers ✦ 1 teaspoon chopped parsley

Cook the butter until it darkens. Slice the brains and pour the butter over them. Keep hot. Put the vinegar and capers in the pan in which the butter cooked. Heat for a moment and pour over the brains. Sprinkle with parsley and serve.

Soufflé de Cervelle Economical

10 oz brains ✦ 2 tablespoons butter ✦ 1 tablespoon flour ✦ 1 glass hot milk ✦ salt and pepper

Poach the blanched brains for 5 minutes and put them through a sieve or blender. Make a sauce with flour, butter and milk and cook it for 10 minutes. Season and lift off the fire.

yolks of 4 eggs	Add the brains and the yolks of egg, stir and cool.
4 whites of egg	Whip the whites until they stand in peaks and fold them into the mixture. Cook the soufflé in a buttered fireproof dish for 40 minutes in a moderate oven (355° F, 180° C, Gas 4). 10 minutes will be enough for individual moulds.

Tongue

For many years tongue was considered the most delicate part of the animal. The story goes that about sixty years ago, travellers arriving at an Argentine *hacienda* were presented with a butcher's knife and the wood necessary to make a great fire. This was an invitation to kill one of the beef cattle and eat it. The visitors showed their appreciation by returning the skin, horns and feet of the animal, and also the tongue, which was considered the choicest part and was reserved for the women and children.

Buying tongue. Ox tongues are sold salted, fresh or smoked. The smoked variety, like all forms of salted tongue, must be soaked for about 12 hours before cooking. When buying an ox tongue see that the skin is smooth. A rough skin is a sign of age. Nowadays ox tongue is often sold 'short cut' with the bone and gristle removed.

A whole ox tongue weighs about 6½ lb; a calf's, 1–2 lb; a pig's tongue, 14–24 oz, and sheep's tongues about 7 oz each. Lamb's tongues are a little smaller. You should allow about 6 oz of raw tongue per person. If tongue is ready-cooked there is no waste and 4–5 oz should be enough.

Though calf's, sheep's, lamb's and pig's tongues are quite good salted and eaten cold, they are more often left unsalted and served hot, braising being one of the best ways of preparing them.

To prepare a tongue. Fresh tongue, after having soaked for 2–3 hours in cold water, will be improved in flavour if you leave it for a day covered with coarse salt.

Smoked tongue should be soaked overnight, and brined or pickled tongue for several hours.

After being poached until it is tender, tongue must be skinned.

To skin a tongue. When the tongue is cooked, let it cool until it is lukewarm. (If it has not been short-cut remove the bone and any surplus fat.) Slit the skin lengthwise on the underside of the tongue and strip it off, being careful not to damage the meat. (Pig's tongues are rather awkward to skin.)

Carving a tongue. The flavour of a tongue depends partly on how it is sliced. Hot tongue, uninteresting if cut into cubes, is excellent in long slices about ¾-inch thick.

Braised Calf's Tongue with Tomatoes Economical

4 oz back pork fat ✦ 2 onions ✦ 1 carrot ✦ a stalk celery ✦ 3 tomatoes ✦ 1 calf's tongue	Put the pork fat in the bottom of a flameproof casserole, covered with chopped vegetables and the tomatoes with skin and pips removed. Lay the tongue on top, cover and cook gently for 10 minutes.
1 glass white wine	Add the wine, raising the heat a little, and reduce by about a quarter with the lid off.
2 glasses bouillon ✦ 3 tablespoons tomato purée 2 cloves garlic, crushed ✦ a bouquet garni ✦ salt and pepper	Stir the tomato purée into the hot bouillon and pour it on to the tongue. Add the garlic and the bouquet garni and season. Close the lid and simmer for 1½ hours. Remove the tongue, skin and slice it and pour over the sauce, which you have put through a sieve.

Sheep's Tongues Economical

4 sheep's tongues, soaked, blanched and trimmed 1 glass white wine ✦ 1 glass bouillon ✦ salt and pepper	Put the tongues into a flameproof casserole with the wine and let it reduce, slowly, by a quarter. Add the hot bouillon. Season.

1 onion ✦ 1 carrot ✦ 2 cloves garlic ✦ a bouquet garni ✦ a branch celery

Cut the vegetables in large pieces and simmer them with the tongues for 1½ hours. Drain the tongues and remove the skins when they are lukewarm. Serve them surrounded by the vegetables and steeped in tomato sauce (p. 203).

Heart

The heart is a muscle which only ceases working at death. It is tasty, cheap and there is very little waste. In proportion to its size, a heart is very heavy.

Choosing a heart. A heart should be a good red. Allow about 6–10 oz for each person according to the amount of stuffing used. Sheep's heart is sometimes sold with the liver, lites (or lungs) and spleen (or melt) which, all together, are called the pluck. Although quite pleasant dishes can be made with the lites and melts they are now usually given to animals, and the liver and heart are sold separately.

How to prepare heart. Before cooking, you should cut a heart in half and remove any clots of blood, little pipes and gristle. Wash the heart carefully in several waters and soak it in cold salted water for at least half an hour. (Ox hearts should be soaked overnight in water to which 1 tablespoon of vinegar to the pint has been added.)

Ox heart must be cooked very slowly and is only fit for braising. Calf's, sheep's and pig's hearts are very good stuffed and roasted, especially if you add extra fat and plenty of herbs to the stuffing. You will need about half a cupful of stuffing for sheep's, lamb's and small calf's hearts. (If you wish to stuff an ox heart before braising you will need four or five times as much.)

Calf's and lamb's hearts can be cut in slices and sautéd. To make the meat more tender, marinate it for half an hour in olive oil with about one-third its volume of lemon juice.

Chinese Heart with Vegetables Very economical

Cut the soaked, trimmed heart and the vegetables in even, fine slices on the bias. See that everything is ready so that you can cook rapidly and without interruption. Sugar peas, which are called in French *pois mange-tout*, have no parchment lining to the pods and so can be eaten entire. Normally the pods are broken into several pieces and cooked in the same way as other green vegetables.

1¼ lb heart ✦ 3 tablespoons flour ✦ ½ cup dried mushrooms ✦ 1 onion ✦ a stalk celery ✦ a handful sugar peas	Roll the sliced heart in flour. Soak the mushrooms in tepid water for ½ hour and slice them.
2 tablespoons lard	Heat the lard to smoking point in a large frying pan and brown the sliced heart and vegetables, shaking the pan continually.
2 teaspoons soya sauce ½ glass hot bouillon ✦ salt and pepper	Add the soya sauce and hot bouillon. Cover and cook gently for 15 minutes. Season and serve with rice.

Stuffed Heart Economical

For this recipe use a small ox or large calf's heart. Prepare it as above but without quite separating the two halves of the heart.

2 shallots ✦ 1 egg ✦ 8 oz sausage meat ✦ 4 tablespoons white breadcrumbs 1 tablespoon chopped fresh herbs ✦ 1 tablespoon brandy ✦ salt and pepper a piece of caul fat (optional)	Chop and mix all the ingredients, including a little of the flesh from inside the heart. Stuff the heart and wrap it in a piece of caul fat or fix it in place with some wooden toothpicks.
3 tablespoons butter	Drench the heart with melted butter and cook in a moderate oven (380° F, 195° C, Gas 5) for 1½ hours, basting frequently.
or	*or*
2 tablespoons flour ½ glass white wine ½ glass hot bouillon	Roll the heart in flour and brown it all over in butter. Moisten with wine and reduce for a few minutes. Add the bouillon, close the lid and simmer for 1½ hours.

Calf's Head, Ears and Feet

Calf's head, ears and feet are excellent and very cheap. However it is wise, when inviting friends, not to experiment with these particular delicacies which, in spite of their undoubted merits, might not be very popular.

Shopping for calf's head, etc. These parts of the animal are usually sold boned and blanched. Sometimes the head, boned and rolled, is sold by weight, and the ears are occasionally prepared separately. The feet can be split and boned.

Both head and feet must be fresh and very white. Don't attempt to keep them more than 48 hours in the refrigerator as they rapidly become limp and gluey.

You should allow about 5½ oz of boned calf's head for each person.

Preparation. However they are to be cooked, calf's head and feet must be carefully washed and any hairs removed. Trim off all the gristle from the nostrils and soak in cold salted water for at least an hour, changing the water from time to time. Then put the head or feet into a saucepan, covered with cold water. Bring to the boil, drain and wash once more. (Make sure, of course, that the butcher has not done all this work for you.)

Remove the bones, rub the head with lemon, and cook it in a '*blanc*' (see below).

Calf's head is very good served cold with vinaigrette, gribiche, rémoulade or poulette sauce (p. 202). The vinegar in the sauce helps to digest the rather gelatinous meat. Calf's head is more digestible when hot and can be served with the brains, prepared separately.

Cooked calf's head is also good sliced, and then fried or grilled.

Calf's feet form the basis of many jellied dishes and are used in certain braises to give them a rich consistency. They can be cooked according to any of the recipes for sheep's or pig's feet or for calf's head.

Frying. Marinate slices of cooked calf's head in 3 parts of oil to 1 part of lemon juice. Dry each piece and dip it in frying batter (p. 177), then plunge the slices into smoking-hot deep fat. Drain well on soft paper.

Grilling. Prepare the slices as above, but instead of dipping them in batter, brush them with melted butter or beaten egg and coat with fine stale breadcrumbs. They can also be dipped in flour or spread with mustard, and sprinkled with melted butter.

Grill the slices gently for 20 minutes, turning once.

A 'Blanc' in which to Boil Calf's Head

The following quantities are sufficient to cook about 1¾ lb of calf's head. Increase proportionately for larger quantities.

about 3½ pints water ✦ 2 tablespoons flour ✦ 1 onion 2 carrots ✦ a stalk celery the white of 2 leeks ✦ 6 peppercorns ✦ 2 cloves 1 lemon ✦ a bouquet garni salt

Mix the flour to a paste and bring it to the boil with the water in a large saucepan. Quarter the lemon and cut the vegetables in pieces and simmer, covered with a cloth, for 15 minutes, together with the seasoning.

Plunge the head in the liquid, which should cover it, and simmer for about 2 hours. When it is done, the bones can easily be detached. Lift out the head and drain it.

To make the head very white, add about 3½ oz beef dripping or lard to the liquid in which it is cooked.

Calf's Head à la Provençale Very economical

1¼ lb calf's head

Cut the blanched calf's head in large pieces and cook it in a '*blanc*' (see above).

2 tablespoons olive oil 3 onions ✦ 3 or 4 tomatoes 2 cloves garlic ✦ salt and pepper

Let the finely chopped onions soften without colouring and add the chopped flesh of the tomatoes. Cook briefly, stir in the crushed garlic and, after a moment or two more cooking, season.

8 black olives ✦ 2 hard-boiled eggs ✦ 1 tablespoon chopped parsley ✦ 1 clove

Put a little of the sauce into a fireproof dish. Add the calf's head sprinkled with lemon juice and surrounded with

chopped garlic ✦ 1 tablespoon olive oil ✦ juice of ½ lemon

sliced eggs and black olives. Cover with the rest of the sauce, dust with parsley and garlic, sprinkle with oil and cook in a moderate oven (380° F, 195° C, Gas 5) for 15 minutes. Serve with small croûtons of fried bread.

If you leave out the garlic and add sliced gherkins, a little tomato purée and some spoonfuls of sherry, this recipe will resemble *tête de veau en tortue*, the classic dish which includes truffles, quenelles, etc.

Stuffed Calf's Feet Very economical

Cook the calf's feet in a *blanc*, cut them open without separating the two halves, and remove the bones. Pig's feet, after being simmered for 4–5 hours, can be cooked in the same way.

The quantities below are for 4 calf's or pig's feet or 8 sheep's trotters:

1 onion ✦ 1 teaspoon oil
½ lb finely minced sausage meat ✦ 2 tablespoons breadcrumbs ✦ 1 tablespoon chopped parsley
1 tablespoon brandy ✦ salt and pepper

Chop the onion finely and soften it in hot oil. Mix together with all the other ingredients including, if you wish, mushrooms sautéd in butter and chopped, or some truffles. Fill each foot with stuffing.

4 pieces of caul fat ✦ 1 egg yolk or some French mustard ✦ breadcrumbs

Soften the caul fat in hot water and wrap it round each foot. Egg-and-breadcrumb them and fry, *or* coat each foot with mustard and breadcrumbs, sprinkle with melted butter and grill.

Pieds de Veau à l'Italienne Economical

Cut the cooked, boned calf's feet into long, narrow strips.

3 or 4 calf's feet ✦ 2 tablespoons oil

Heat the oil to smoking point in a flameproof casserole and fry the strips of meat lightly.

1 onion ✦ 1 carrot ✦ a stalk celery ✦ 1 clove garlic

Chop the vegetables as finely as possible (or put them through a Mouli) and let them colour with the meat.

1 tablespoon flour ✦ ½ glass white wine	Sprinkle with flour, moisten with wine and simmer gently, stirring all the time, until the sauce has thickened.
1 teaspoon grated orange rind ✦ 1 teaspoon grated lemon rind ✦ a bouquet garni ✦ salt and pepper	Add all the seasoning.
½ glass water ✦ 3 tablespoons tomato purée	Dilute the tomato purée in water, pour it into the casserole and stir. Cover and simmer for ½ hour. Remove the bouquet and serve.

Pig's Head, Ears, Trotters and Tails

All these bits and pieces of pig are extremely cheap and make tasty dishes, but they are not easy to buy. Most butchers will produce them for you with a few days' notice, either fresh or salted. If you are in a hurry, try the butcher's shops round the big markets. These usually carry a stock of the more plebeian, but delightful extremities of the various animals.

All these pieces must be carefully cleaned and blanched in the same way as calf's head (p. 184). Whether boiled, stewed or braised they must only simmer gently. Allow 1–1½ hours for pig's ears, 2 hours for tails and 5 hours for trotters (so that the bones are really tender and can be crunched).

The preparation and cooking of pig's head, etc. are the same as those we have described for calf and the same recipes can be used. The classic English cookery books contain excellent recipes for brawn and so on. We only add two recipes for pig's ears which are typically French.

Braised Pig's Ears Very economical

4 pig's ears	Clean and singe the ears and plunge them into a large saucepan of boiling water. After 5 minutes, lift them out, drain and cut in half lengthwise.
8 oz sliced back pork fat 1 carrot ✦ a stalk celery ✦ a bouquet garni	Line a flameproof casserole with pork fat covered with chopped vegetables and lay the ears, flat, on top. Add the bouquet, cover, and simmer for 5 minutes.

Ingredients	Method
1 glass white wine	Pour in the wine and cook, gently, with the lid off until the wine is reduced almost completely.
1 tablespoon flour ✦ 1 glass bouillon ✦ salt and pepper	Sprinkle with flour, stir in the hot bouillon, season and cook, with the lid off, over a low fire for another hour. Lift out the ears and keep hot. Strain the contents of the casserole and let them reduce to half over the fire. Serve this sauce separately.

Oreilles à la Lyonnaise Very economical

Boil the ears and put them to cool beneath a weighted plate, then cut them in long strips about ½-inch wide.

Ingredients	Method
4 ears ✦ 2 tablespoons fat 3 or 4 onions	Brown the sliced onions in hot fat. Add the ears and sauter all together for a few minutes.
salt and pepper ✦ 2 tablespoons vinegar ✦ 1 teaspoon chopped parsley	Season, sprinkle with vinegar, heat for a moment or two and serve, dusted with parsley.

Tripe

The French make a distinction between '*tripes*', which consists of all four stomachs of the ox, and '*gras-double*', the three stomachs sold here as tripe.

Tripe is usually sold blanched and partially cooked, after which only from 1–1½ hours' further cooking is necessary.

Cooked with care and affection tripe makes a wonderful dish but it has lost its popularity—probably through the bitter memories of old-fashioned nursery meals and platefuls of grey, slippery shapes looking like something out of an underwater film. It would be difficult to imagine any relationship between these horrors and *tripes à la mode de Caen*, a fragrant mixture of vegetables, herbs, ox feet and tripe sealed into an earthenware pot with cider and calvados, and slowly richening in a gentle heat. Some rather simpler recipes follow.

Grilled Tripe Very economical

Ingredients	Method
1½ lb cooked tripe ✦ 2–3 tablespoons flour ✦ 3	Cut the tripe in pieces, dip them in flour, sprinkle with oil and coat with

tablespoons oil ✦ breadcrumbs

breadcrumbs. Grill gently for 4–5 minutes each side. Season, and serve with quarters of lemon.

Tripe is excellent coated with egg and breadcrumbs and deep-fried.

Gras-Double à la Lyonnaise Very economical

Cut the cooked tripe in fairly wide strips. Dry them carefully.

1½ lb cooked tripe ✦ 3 tablespoons fat ✦ 4–5 onions

Brown the tripe in hot fat. Add the sliced onions and sauter all together for 15 minutes.

salt and pepper ✦ 2 tablespoons vinegar ✦ 1 tablespoon chopped parsley

Season, sprinkle with vinegar, dust with parsley and serve.

Gras-Double à l'Italienne Economical

½ glass olive oil ✦ 4 oz pig's flare fat ✦ 1 onion a bay leaf ✦ 1½ lb partly-cooked tripe ✦ 3 tomatoes

Heat the oil and fat in a large flameproof casserole and brown the finely-chopped onions. Cut the tripe in fine strips and add them, together with the chopped tomato pulp and the bay leaf.

1 glass white wine ✦ 3 tablespoons tomato purée 4 cloves crushed garlic ✦ a pinch rosemary in a muslin bag ✦ salt and pepper 1 glass hot water

Moisten with wine, add the tomato purée, rosemary and seasoning. Close the casserole and let it simmer for 1½ hours, adding water when necessary. The sauce must remain thick.

1 tablespoon chopped parsley ✦ 2 cloves garlic (optional)

Remove the bay leaf and rosemary. Serve, sprinkled with chopped parsley and garlic and decorated with small croûtons of fried bread.

Gras-Double à la Polonaise Very economical

1½ lb cooked tripe ✦ 2 tablespoons fat ✦ salt and pepper

Slice the tripe very finely. Heat the fat and brown the tripe in a frying pan. Lift it out and season.

juice of ½ lemon ✦ 1 chopped hard-boiled egg

Put the tripe, sharpened with lemon juice, into a buttered fireproof dish.

1 tablespoon chopped parsley ✦ 1 tablespoon breadcrumbs ✦ 2 tablespoons melted butter

Sprinkle it in turn with egg, parsley, breadcrumbs and melted butter and brown it for 10 minutes in a very hot oven (445° F, 230° C, Gas 8) or under the grill.

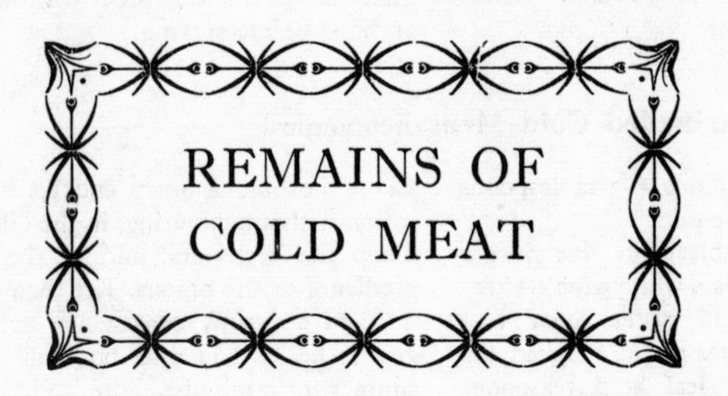

REMAINS OF COLD MEAT

A ROAST or a braise is always more successful if it is of generous proportions. Any remains can be eaten cold with a variety of salads, or you can warm it up in a number of different ways.

Remains of beef, veal and pork can be minced and mixed with each other or with fresh meat, ham, sausage meat, breadcrumbs and so on to form all sorts of delightful dishes. (Mutton has rather a strong flavour and is not a very good mixer.)

However you decide to use your leftovers make sure that they are presented agreeably and with plenty of variation: on fried croûtons, for example, in scallop shells, or as sizzling golden-brown *gratinés*.

Here are some ideas which may suggest further combinations:

Sliced Cold Meat in Tomato Sauce Economical

This tomato sauce does not require cooking.

2 tomatoes	Remove the skin and pips and chop the pulp of the tomatoes.
1 clove garlic, crushed ✦ 1 tablespoon chopped parsley, chervil and fresh basil ✦ ½ glass olive oil ✦ salt and freshly-milled pepper ✦ 1 tablespoon wine vinegar ✦ 1 teaspoon grated lemon rind	Mix all these ingredients with the chopped tomato and stand them, in a covered bowl, for several hours in a cool place.

1 lb or so cold cooked meat	Slice the meat and cover it with sauce an hour before serving.

Marinaded Cold Meat Economical

2 onions ✦ 3 tablespoons olive oil	Chop the onions finely and let them soften without colouring, in the oil.
1 tablespoon wine vinegar 1 glass white wine ✦ 1 teaspoon caster sugar ✦ 2 cloves garlic, crushed ✦ a bay leaf ✦ 2 teaspoons parsley, chervil, sage, rosemary and basil ✦ 1 glass bouillon	Chop the herbs and add all the ingredients to the onions. Let them reduce to a syrupy consistency over a gentle heat. Add the bouillon and simmer for 5 minutes more.
remains of cold meat	Lay the sliced meat in a deep dish. Cover it with hot sauce and marinate for about 12 hours. Lift out the meat and serve it with gherkins, olives and pickles.

Sliced Meat with Piquant Sauce Economical

3 onions ✦ 1 tablespoon oil ✦ 1 tablespoon flour 1 glass bouillon	Soften the chopped onions in hot oil without letting them brown. Sprinkle with flour and stir in the bouillon, little by little.
1 tablespoon vinegar ✦ salt and pepper ✦ 1 clove garlic, crushed ✦ a bay leaf ✦ a pinch sugar	Add the rest of the ingredients and cook very gently for 10 minutes (with a little more bouillon if the sauce becomes too thick).
1 teaspoon capers ✦ 1 tablespoon French mustard ✦ thinly sliced cold meat	Lift the sauce from the fire, remove the bay leaf and add the capers. Pour half the sauce into a buttered fireproof dish. Lay the slices of meat, overlapping, in the dish and cover with the rest of the sauce.
2 tablespoons browned breadcrumbs ✦ 1 tablespoon melted butter	Sprinkle with breadcrumbs and melted butter and cook for 20 minutes in an oven pre-heated to 380° F, (195° C, Gas 5).

Les Restes de Viande Provençale Economical

2 aubergines ✦ coarse salt	Cut the aubergines in lengthwise slices, rub them with salt and let the juice exude for 15 minutes. Dry them carefully.
3 tablespoons olive oil	Fry the aubergine slices in olive oil. Drain them carefully and arrange them in a buttered fireproof dish.
4 oz unsmoked bacon ✦ 3 small onions ✦ remains of cold meat	Brown the diced bacon and quartered onions in the frying pan. Cut the meat in small strips and lay it, mixed with bacon and onions, on the aubergines.
3 or 4 tomatoes ✦ 2 cloves garlic ✦ salt and pepper 1 tablespoon chopped parsley	Slice the flesh of the tomatoes and fry them in the pan, adding oil if necessary. Add the chopped garlic and parsley and cook for a minute or two. Season and pour over the meat.
2 tablespoons browned breadcrumbs ✦ 2 tablespoons melted butter	Sprinkle with breadcrumbs and melted butter and brown as above for 20 minutes.

Minced Meat on Croûtons Very economical

For this dish you will find that onion goes better with beef, and garlic with mutton.

1 onion *or* 1 clove garlic 1½ cups minced cold meat 1 tablespoon chopped fresh herbs ✦ salt and pepper	Chop the onion or garlic and mix with the meat, herbs and seasoning.
1 tablespoon butter ✦ 1 tablespoon oil ✦ 2 teaspoons flour ✦ ½ glass hot bouillon ✦ 1 tablespoon tomato purée (optional)	Heat the oil and butter and fry the meat for a moment over lively heat. Reduce the temperature and sprinkle the meat with flour. Stir in the bouillon, with the tomato purée if you wish, and cook for 10 minutes.
4 slices bread ✦ butter 4 poached eggs	Fry the slices of bread in butter, after removing the crusts. Pile mince on each croûton and put an egg on top.

Picadillo Economical

This Cuban dish should be accompanied by boiled rice, fried bananas and fried eggs.

2 onions ✦ 2 green peppers ✦ 2 tablespoons oil 1 clove garlic, crushed	Remove the seeds from the peppers and chop them with the onions and garlic. Let them soften in the oil, without colouring.
3 tomatoes ✦ a bay leaf 1 clove	Add the chopped tomato pulp, clove and bay leaf and cook for 10 minutes. Remove the bay leaf and clove.
2 cups minced cold meat ½ cup bouillon ✦ salt and pepper ✦ 1 teaspoon vinegar	Stir in the meat and pour the mixture into a buttered fireproof dish. Sprinkle with bouillon and vinegar and season. Bake in a hot oven (425° F, 220° C, Gas 7) for 20 minutes.

Fricadelles Very economical

2 onions ✦ 1 tablespoon butter ✦ 4 cooked potatoes	Soften the onions in butter. Mash the potatoes in a large bowl and add the onions.
2 cups cold minced meat 1 egg ✦ 1 teaspoon each chopped parsley and chervil ✦ salt and pepper nutmeg	Mix all together with the ingredients in the bowl and form 8 meat balls. Flatten them slightly.
2 tablespoons flour ✦ 2 or 3 tablespoons fat	Dip the fricadelles in flour and brown them in very hot fat for 5 minutes on each side. Serve with tomato or chasseur sauce (pp 200 and 203).

Gratin of Meat with Cabbage Very economical

1 white cabbage ✦ salt and pepper	Cut the cabbage in four and remove the stalk. Cook for 20 minutes, salted and peppered. Drain well and chop coarsely.
1 clove garlic ✦ 1 tablespoon fat or lard ✦ 2 cups minced cold meat ✦ 3 tablespoons tomato purée	Chop the garlic and brown it lightly in a saucepan. Add the meat and tomato purée. Sprinkle with flour and moisten with bouillon. Mix in the cabbage, season and cook over a low fire for 10 minutes.
3 tablespoons breadcrumbs ✦ 1 tablespoon melted butter	Put the mixture into a buttered fireproof dish, sprinkle with breadcrumbs and butter and brown in a hot oven or under the grill for 10–15 minutes.

Minced Meat with Chestnuts Economical

For suggestions on how to peel chestnuts see p. 134. Cover the peeled chestnuts with cold water or bouillon and season them. Add a stalk of celery, bring them to the boil, and cook gently for $\frac{1}{2}$ hour. Let them cool in their own liquid.

1 tablespoon butter ✦ 1 or 2 onions ✦ 3 tablespoons tomato purée ✦ 1 glass bouillon ✦ salt and pepper	Heat the butter in a saucepan and soften the chopped onions. Stir in the tomato purée and bouillon, and season.
2 cups cold minced meat about 20 cooked chestnuts	Add the meat and the chestnuts, broken in pieces and continue to cook gently, without allowing the mixture to boil.
4 tablespoons fresh cream	Stir in the cream and serve the mince in a deep dish.

As the chestnuts are filling, they replace potatoes. Serve with a green vegetable or a salad.

Minced Meat with Macaroni Very economical

This dish should really be made with *lasagne* which are wide strips of paste, but you can use macaroni or noodles instead. Remains of beef, veal or pork are suitable.

1$\frac{1}{2}$ cups minced cold meat 2 slices ham	Mix the meat and chopped ham.
1 egg ✦ 2 tablespoons grated parmesan ✦ 2, or more, tablespoons bouillon ✦ 3 tablespoons breadcrumbs ✦ salt and pepper	Mix all together in a bowl with the meat, using enough bouillon to keep the mixture soft.
$\frac{1}{2}$ lb pasta	Cook the pasta in plenty of boiling, salted water until it is just tender. Drain and arrange in layers in a buttered fireproof dish, alternately with the meat. The top layer should be pasta.
3 tablespoons melted butter	Sprinkle with melted butter and cook for $\frac{1}{2}$ hour in a moderate oven (380° F, 195° C, Gas 5). Serve with tomato sauce (p. 203) and grated cheese.

You can, if you prefer, butter a mould and sprinkle it with breadcrumbs, and then cook the mixture in a bain-marie for ¾ hour, covered with buttered greaseproof paper. Wait 10 minutes before turning out the mould.

Cooked Meat Soufflé with Mushroom Sauce

Moderately expensive

This soufflé can be made with the remains of roast beef or pork, veal, chicken or ham.

2 tablespoons butter ✦ 10 mushrooms ✦ 3 tablespoons flour ✦ 2 cups milk	Chop the mushrooms and soften them in butter. Sprinkle with flour and stir in the milk, a little at a time, being careful to avoid lumps. Cook gently for 10 minutes and when the sauce is thick, lift it from the fire.
2 cups minced cold meat 4 eggs	Add the meat, season, and stir in the egg yolks. Let the mixture cool. Whip the whites of egg stiffly and fold them in. Pour the mixture into a buttered soufflé dish and bake in a low oven (310° F, 155° C, Gas 2) for 40 minutes.

Meanwhile, prepare the mushroom sauce.

1 tablespoon butter ✦ 12 mushrooms ✦ 2 tablespoons flour ✦ 1½ glasses bouillon ✦ salt and pepper 2 tablespoons cream minced parsley	Brown the sliced mushrooms in butter. Sift in the flour and stir in the bouillon. Season and cook for 10 minutes. At the moment of serving add the cream and heat without boiling. Dust with parsley.

Cold Tongue à la Diable Economical

8 slices tongue ✦ 3 tablespoons French mustard a pinch cayenne	Mix cayenne and mustard and spread the slices on each side.
6 tablespoons white breadcrumbs	Coat the tongue with breadcrumbs, pressing them on with the back of a spoon.
3 tablespoons melted butter	Drizzle with melted butter and brown on both sides in the oven or under the grill.

Miroton de Bœuf Economical

Miroton de bœuf resembles *bœuf Lyonnaise* but it takes more time to prepare. In compensation, it needs less meat. Use the remains of braised or boiled beef.

3 onions ✦ 1 tablespoon fat ✦ 1 tablespoon flour 3 tablespoons tomato purée *or* 2 tomatoes ✦ ½–1 glass bouillon ✦ 1 tablespoon vinegar	Brown the finely-sliced onions in fat. Sprinkle with flour and allow it to colour slightly. Add the fresh tomatoes and ½ glass of bouillon, or tomato purée and 1 glass of bouillon, and the vinegar and seasoning. Cook 10 minutes over a low fire.
remains of beef ✦ 1 teaspoon chopped parsley	Cut the meat in fine slices and heat it gently in the sauce. Sprinkle with parsley and serve.

If you prefer, put everything into a buttered fireproof dish. Surround it with mashed potato (piped into a pattern if you wish to be elegant), sprinkle with breadcrumbs and melted butter, and brown in the oven or under the grill for 10 minutes.

SAUCES

A SIZZLING steak bathed in its own rich juices with a pat of fresh butter slowly melting on top is a perfect dish. But what about the sad slices of cold meat left from Sunday's joint, or the drab, tweedy look of the boiled beef from the *pot-au-feu*?

This is where a spicy sauce, like a pretty hat, will lift your morale on wings and bring delight to your family and friends.

Here are a few such sauces:

Béarnaise Sauce

Béarnaise sauce is delicious, but not too easy to make. If overheated, it turns into scrambled eggs—if the butter is added too quickly the sauce remains liquid.

It is very important that the water in the bain-marie (p. 34) should only just boil and the temperature of the sauce itself must never exceed 175° F (80° C). (For this reason it is dangerous to make it in a double saucepan as the water in the outer pan can so easily boil too hard without your noticing it.)

The butter must be ready cut in dice before you put the saucepan into the bain-marie, as from now on you must not stop stirring for a moment.

A small wire whisk and a copper saucepan (or bowl) which spreads the heat evenly will help you to make a perfect béarnaise sauce.

2 shallots ✦ 1 tablespoon minced parsley and chervil ✦ a glass dry white wine ✦ salt and pepper 1 tablespoon cold water 2 yolks of egg ✦ about 6 oz butter	Put the shallots, herbs, wine and seasoning into a small saucepan and let them reduce, as slowly as possible, until only about 2 tablespoons of liquid are left. Strain the liquid into a small bowl. Add the water, egg yolks and a nut of butter. Whisk them well together and put the saucepan into a bain-marie. As soon as the mixture begins to thicken, add the rest of the butter, a little at a time, whisking as you do so.
2 teaspoons chopped chervil and tarragon ✦ lemon juice	As soon as the sauce is thick and creamy add the herbs, sharpen it with lemon juice, and serve.

Bercy Butter

3 shallots ✦ 2 teaspoons butter	Melt the butter in a small saucepan and let the chopped shallots soften, but not take colour.
½ glass white wine ✦ salt and pepper	Add the wine and let it reduce over the fire until the sauce has the consistency of a syrup. Season.
3½ oz butter ✦ 1 tablespoon lemon juice ✦ 1 teaspoon chopped parsley and chervil	Soften the butter and mix it, off the fire, with the shallots. Add the lemon juice and herbs.

Slices of bone marrow poached in salted water make a delicious garnish for meat served with Bercy butter.

Bordelaise Sauce

3 shallots ✦ a stalk celery 1 small carrot ✦ a pinch thyme ✦ half a bay leaf	Chop the vegetables finely and put them into a small saucepan with the herbs. Add the butter and heat gently without letting them colour.
1 teaspoon flour ✦ 1 glass red wine ✦ ½ glass bouillon	Sift in the flour, mix well, and stir in the wine. Let it reduce gently to about one-third. Add the bouillon and cook for 10 minutes more, stirring all the time.
3 tablespoons butter	Put the sauce through a fine sieve, stir in the butter, and serve.

Sauce Chasseur

2 shallots ✦ 2 teaspoons butter ✦ 4 or 5 mushrooms	Soften the chopped shallots in butter without letting them colour. Add the finely-sliced mushrooms and soften them too.
2 teaspoons flour ✦ 1 glass white wine ✦ 1 teaspoon tomato purée	When the mushrooms are just beginning to brown, stir in the flour. Add the wine, being careful to avoid lumps, and reduce it to half. Stir in the tomato purée.
$1\frac{1}{2}$ glasses bouillon ✦ salt and pepper	Moisten slowly with warm bouillon and simmer very gently for 15 minutes. Season.
1 teaspoon each chopped parsley and chervil	Just before serving, add the herbs.

Sauce Gribiche

1 yolk hard-boiled egg 1 raw yolk ✦ 2 teaspoons light French mustard	Pound the two yolks of eggs in a mortar or bowl. Add the mustard and make a smooth paste.
1 glass oil	Add the oil little by little as if you were making mayonnaise.
1 teaspoon vinegar ✦ 1 teaspoon chopped parsley salt and pepper	Complete the sauce by stirring in the vinegar, herbs and seasoning.

Horse-radish Sauce

Horse-radish, say the gardeners, is enough to make you weep. Once allow it to grow and you will never get rid of it.

Whether this is true or not we have never discovered, but it does bring tears to the eyes of a cook, and some people find grating horse-radish even more painful than peeling onions.

Many shops sell jars of grated horse-radish. This makes quite a pleasant change from mustard. It is also very good stirred into thick cream and iced, or added to a hot white sauce. Here are two versions of horse-radish sauce, one hot and one cold. Either is excellent with cold or boiled meats.

Hot

3 tablespoons butter ✦ 3 tablespoons flour ✦ 2	Warm the flour and butter together without allowing them to brown. Stir

glasses milk ✦ salt and pepper
2 tablespoons grated horse-radish ✦ ½ teaspoon vinegar ✦ 1 tablespoon cream ✦ ½ teaspoon caster sugar

in the milk little by little and cook gently for 15 minutes. Season.
Mix the horse-radish and vinegar, and add them to the sauce with the cream and sugar. Heat through, without allowing the sauce to boil.

Cold

3 tablespoons grated horse-radish ✦ 1 slice white bread ✦ 2 tablespoons milk ✦ 5 oz fresh cream ✦ 1 teaspoon lemon juice ✦ salt ✦ a pinch sugar ✦ ½ cup chopped walnuts (optional)

Soak the bread in milk, crumble and mix with the horse-radish. Season. Stir in the fresh cream and lemon juice. Chill the sauce before serving.

Madeira Sauce

3 shallots ✦ 1 rasher bacon
1 tablespoon butter ✦ 2 teaspoons flour ✦ 1 tablespoon chopped mushroom
1 teaspoon tomato purée
1 cup bouillon ✦ 1 teaspoon chopped fresh herbs
1 glass madeira or sherry

Brown the chopped shallots and bacon in butter. Sprinkle with flour and let it colour. Add the tomato purée, mushroom and bouillon and bring to the boil. Cook for 15 minutes. Season. Add the herbs and cook 5 minutes more.

Heat the madeira or sherry and reduce on the fire for 2 minutes. Add to the sauce and simmer until it reaches the consistency of syrup.

Maître d'hôtel Butter

3 tablespoons butter ✦ 2 teaspoons chopped parsley and chervil ✦ 1 teaspoon lemon juice ✦ 1 teaspoon light French mustard ✦ salt and pepper

Soften the butter and work it lightly together with the herbs and seasoning. Put a pat of maître d'hôtel butter on each portion of meat and decorate the dish with watercress.

Maître d'hôtel butter can be made in advance and kept in

the refrigerator. It is then easily cut into pats and put on top of the sizzling hot meat just before it is served.

Sauce Mornay

½ pint béchamel sauce 4–5 tablespoons grated cheese ✦ 1 small teaspoon French mustard ✦ pepper and salt ✦ 2 tablespoons cream (optional)

As the cheese will thicken, the béchamel sauce should be rather thin. Stir the cheese and seasonings into the hot sauce and re-heat carefully, never allowing it to boil, or the sauce will curdle. Add the cream, if you wish, at the last moment.

Mustard Sauce

This sauce goes very well with cold beef. The oil can be replaced by a glass of fresh cream and in this case use lemon instead of vinegar.

3 tablespoons light French mustard ✦ ½ glass olive oil (or cream)

Put the mustard in a small bowl and pour the oil down the side, drop by drop, stirring all the time as if you were making a mayonnaise.

½ teaspoon wine vinegar (or lemon juice) ✦ salt a pinch cayenne ✦ 1 teaspoon minced parsley

When the sauce is smooth and thick add the vinegar and seasoning and, finally, the chopped parsley.

Sauce Poulette

3 tablespoons butter ✦ 2 tablespoons flour ✦ 1 cup bouillon ✦ ½ teaspoon lemon juice ✦ salt and pepper.

Blend the butter and flour over low heat. Stir in the bouillon and cook for 10 minutes. When the sauce is syrupy add the lemon juice and season.

1 large teaspoon finely chopped parsley ✦ a pinch chopped savory ✦ 1 dessertspoon mushroom juice (optional)

Add the herbs and flavouring to the sauce and bring to the boil again. Add more lemon juice if required.

1 egg yolk ✦ 2 tablespoons cream

Mix the egg and cream and stir into the sauce, being careful not to let it boil. Heat for a few moments, and serve.

Sauce Remoulade

½ pint mayonnaise ✦ 1 teaspoon each chopped capers, gherkins, parsley, chervil and tarragon, English and French mustard ✦ 1 teaspoon anchovy essence *or* 2 pounded fillets anchovy

Stir all the ingredients together and mix them into the mayonnaise. You may care to add a little extra mustard.

Tarragon Sauce

4 or 5 tablespoons butter
1 or 2 egg yolks ✦ 2 tablespoons French mustard
1 tablespoon wine vinegar
½ teaspoon powdered dried tarragon ✦ 2 tablespoons cream ✦ salt and pepper
1 tablespoon chopped fresh tarragon and chives

Put the eggs and mustard into a bowl and mix in the butter, which has been softened until it is almost melted. When the mixture is well blended stir in the vinegar, tarragon and cream, one after the other. Season, and add the herbs.

The sauce may be served cold, or heated in a bain-marie, taking care that the water does not boil.

Tomato Sauce

1 tablespoon fat or butter
1 carrot ✦ a stalk celery
1 tablespoon flour
4 tomatoes and a tablespoon tomato purée *or* 5 tablespoons purée
1½ glasses bouillon ✦ a bouquet garni ✦ salt and pepper ✦ a pinch sugar

Chop the vegetables and soften them for a few minutes in the hot fat. Dredge with flour and let it just colour.
Remove the skin and pips from the tomatoes and chop them in large pieces.
Stir the bouillon into the vegetable pan together with tomatoes, purée, herbs and seasoning. Close the lid and simmer for 1 hour, adding more liquid if necessary. (If the sauce is too thin, remove the lid and let it reduce.) Put the sauce through a fine sieve or an electric blender.

Vinaigrette Sauce

½ cup oil ✦ 3 tablespoons vinegar ✦ ½ teaspoon capers ✦ ½ teaspoon each finely chopped parsley, chives, tarragon and chervil ✦ salt and pepper

Mix all together.

You can also add ½ teaspoon finely chopped onion, ½ teaspoon French mustard and even some chopped hard-boiled egg.

INDEX

(A) RECIPES: GROUPED ACCORDING TO COST

1. Expensive

2. Moderately expensive

3. Economical

(B) GENERAL INDEX

INDEX